Praise for
The Top Ten Things Dead People Want to Tell YOU

"A book about living that will help readers see more beauty, feel more power, and know more love."

— **don Miguel Ruiz**, international best-selling author of *The Four Agreements*

"Fabulous! Mike Dooley shows you how to stay alive for the whole of your life . . . and beyond!"

— **Robert Holden**, Ph.D., author of *Holy Shift!*

"Three times, from three completely independent sources, I was told, 'You need to meet Mike Dooley.' After the fourth time, when the person doing the suggesting even went to the trouble to forward his e-mail, I took it as an omen. To all four of you who thought I should meet this incredible writer, this awesome spokesman for the Universe, for joy, and now for all our dead ancestors, I owe you. For everybody else, don't wait. Get *The Top Ten Things Dead People Want to Tell YOU* and everything else Mike Dooley has ever written and read it now."

— **Pam Grout**, #1 *New York Times* best-selling author of *E-Squared* and *E-Cubed*

"Mike Dooley has penned a brilliant, deep, and at times hilarious account of life—and life after life. Read it cover to cover and don't miss a page. If you've ever wondered about the nature of reality, how consciousness creates the world we live in, and the truth about time and space, this book will ring bells in your DNA and wake you up to live with joyful awareness. Read it with an open mind and be prepared to have all your preconceptions challenged with a smile and a wink. Bottom line—you won't be the same person who began it when you've savored the last page. I loved it!"

— **Colette Baron-Reid**, author of *The Map, Messages from Spirit*, and best-selling oracle cards *Wisdom of the Hidden Realms* and *Wisdom of Avalon*

"In *The Top Ten Things Dead People Want to Tell YOU*, Mike Dooley lifts the veil between our perceptual world and the world beyond our physical sight. Mike reminds us that we're always being guided. His assurance is the greatest gift we can receive, as it helps us accept that we are not alone. Read this book and reconnect with the love that is all around you."

— **Gabrielle Bernstein**, *New York Times* best-selling author of *Miracles Now*

"I love this book! Page after page, I found myself going, 'Well, that explains things!' and feeling inspired, full of joy, and wanting more. Who knew 'Dead People' could be so smart? A must read!"

— **Nick Ortner**, *New York Times* best-selling author of *The Tapping Solution*

"Mike Dooley has written a refreshing, powerful, and paradigm-shifting book! *The Top Ten Things Dead People Want to Tell YOU* will give you a new understanding of the important people in your life who have passed on, and also will inspire you to live your life to the fullest while you're still here in body on earth."

— **Mike Robbins**, author of *Nothing Changes Until You Do*

"There are those we will meet lifetime after lifetime, and not birth nor death will truly separate us. This book is your friend in the discovery of all that lies beneath and beyond."

— **Katherine Fugate**, screenwriter

the
top
ten
things
dead people
want
to
tell
YOU

ALSO BY MIKE DOOLEY

Dreams Come True

Leveraging the Universe

Manifesting Change

Infinite Possibilities

Choose Them Wisely

Even More Notes from the Universe

More Notes from the Universe

Notes from the Universe

An Adventurer's Guide to the Jungles of Time and Space

Totally Unique Thoughts

Please visit:

Hay House USA: www.hayhouse.com®
Hay House Australia: www.hayhouse.com.au
Hay House UK: www.hayhouse.co.uk
Hay House India: www.hayhouse.co.in

the
top
ten
things
dead people
want
to
tell

YOU

MIKE DOOLEY

HAY HOUSE, INC.
Carlsbad, California • New York City
London • Sydney • New Delhi

Published in the United States by: Hay House, Inc.: www.hayhouse.com®
Published in Australia by: Hay House Australia Pty. Ltd.: www.hayhouse.com.au
Published in the United Kingdom by: Hay House UK, Ltd.: www.hayhouse.co.uk
Published in India by: Hay House Publishers India: www.hayhouse.co.in

Cover design: Charles McStravick • *Interior design:* Riann Bender

The author of this book does not dispense medical advice or prescribe the
use of any technique as a form of treatment for physical, emotional, or medical
problems without the advice of a physician, either directly or indirectly. The intent of the author is only to offer information of a general nature to help you in
your quest for emotional and spiritual well-being. In the event you use any of the
information in this book for yourself, the author and the publisher assume no
responsibility for your actions.

Library of Congress Cataloging-in-Publication Data

Dooley, Mike
  The top ten things dead people want to tell you / Mike Dooley. -- 1st Edition.
      pages cm
  ISBN 978-1-4019-4555-8 (tradepaper : alk. paper) 1. Life--Miscellanea. 2. Dead-
-Miscellanea. 3. Future life--Miscellanea. I. Title.
  BD431.D685 2014
  128--dc23
                                    2014013404

Tradepaper ISBN: 978-1-4019-4555-8

13 12 11 10 9 8 7 6 5
1st edition, January 2016

Printed in the United States of America

To the living—it's still your turn

Contents

Introduction

No one knows how it all began, not even the dead, but everyone knows that it did.

Fortunately, no one needs to know to nevertheless begin living deliberately, drawing more fun and happiness into their lives. Unfortunately, however, this isn't nearly as apparent to the living as it is to the dead, *these days*. There are far more advanced civilizations spread throughout the cosmos, including our world in times to come (the future), in which the living know just as much as the dead—about all things. Right now, however, for reasons that will soon become clear as you make your way through these pages, the dead have a hugely improved perspective. They see more. They remember choosing their lives. They remember the love—inescapable, caressing, and sublime. Thus, they have something to say to the living, who presently know none of this.

These are very primitive times, which makes the top ten things the dead have to tell you all the more pressing.

How do I know?

I just do. In the same way you know you're loved without even hearing it. And you'll understand more as we go along.

How we know what we know is not quite as important as *that* we know it, right? As long as it's the truth. Just like you don't have to know who turned on a light in a darkened room to make use of that light.

This is the case, of course, with the truth concerning life and death. It doesn't matter how many opinions there are of it; the truth is what it is. And it doesn't matter how you find it, just that you do, and the sooner you do, the greater your peace. The way you'll know it's the truth is that it'll make sense—logically, intellectually, and emotionally—which isn't too often the case given the versions of it that've been tossed about in recent millennia. Finding it, you'll feel liberated, empowered, clear, joyful, loving, your confusion banished. And then suddenly you'll see its evidence everywhere, even right under your very nose, *including* your nose itself. Plus, you'll probably happy dance—a lot.

DANCING IN THE TRUTH OF LOVE

Happy feet on? Because this book is about dancing in the truth of love that you've silently felt your whole life.

Fear not, I won't ask you to make any huge leaps of blind faith to keep up with my explanations. Instead I'll share all that I've come to know with a bit of logic and common sense, now and in the chapters that follow. For starters:

+ If you thought, as all mainstream quantum physicists do, that time and space are illusionary, and

+ If you believe, as do 92 percent[1] of the living, that we survive our own physical death, then

= Wouldn't you expect the dead to be *extremely anxious* to reach out to comfort and inspire those they love and humanity at large?

You answered yes, right? You'd obviously expect that after having just traversed their own mortality from cradle to grave, with the absolutely stunning realization of their continued existence—with personality and sense of humor intact—they'd want to shout it from the mountaintops. Finding that in spite of their own sins and embarrassing faux pas, they're bathed in love and have a vastly improved view of what life is all about, they'd naturally want to "shake their tail feathers" for us.

Imagine being the dearly departed loved one yourself, post–after party, taking a peek back down on earth, happy tears still wet on your cheeks, and seeing the heartbreak and bedlam among the grieving left in your wake. *Shiver me timbers!* Suddenly nothing would be more important than reaching back. To tell them it's okay! *All is supremely well! You're not dead! You'll meet up later! It's still their turn! Keep on dreaming! Keep on living! Keep on loving!*

And wouldn't receiving such news fantastically change everything for the living, forever? And who

---

1   According to a 2007 Pew study.

better to calm the bereaved and inspire all of us than those we love and miss?

What's Not God?

The compulsion of the "dead" to reach out intensifies when they discover there's no trace of a God in the afterlife *as depicted by nearly every religion.* Which is really great news when you consider how most religions depict God. Of course *there is a God*, just not like the one taught by the blind who lead the blind. Words sometimes slip when we try to apply them to truth, but to approximate: God is the sum of *all that is*—every voice, every heartbeat, every man, woman, and child, every animal, every insect, every boulder, planet, and mote of dust, including sentient beings far removed from time and space. "What's *not* God?" might be asked to simplify the answer: "Nothing."

You're getting this, aren't you? It's what you suspected all along. We do know the truth when we meet it because it runs in our blood and forms our DNA. And so, when we ponder great questions or hear new ideas, we can, if we're ready, finally allow ourselves to remember it. The truth *is* who and what we are, neither abstract nor fleeting; we are "it" come alive. *It's objective.* Real. Simple. And while there may be an infinite number of roads to Rome, none of them changes Rome.

We know the truth when we meet it. It's just that having taken the plunge into "life" ourselves in this early stage of our civilization's spiritual development, we don't usually grant ourselves permission to go to places in thought that we can't touch, taste, see, hear, or feel.

Very *caveman*, yet very predictable for where we are in our evolutionary arc.

These *are* primitive times, and given that times are defined by the people who occupy them, we are primitive people. Not by chance, though, but by design. We knew it would be like this. We chose to show up early in humanity's development, perhaps as part of the price for getting to show up later as masters, or because the possibilities that exist today won't exist in the same way later on. Doesn't really matter now; we're here. Babes in the jungles of time and space, and therefore understandably scared by the world around us, feeling vulnerable, relying almost exclusively on our physical senses to label, define, and make progress. E-w-w-w-w... and ouch!

> While there may be an infinite number of roads to Rome, none of them changes Rome.

If It's Broken, Fix It

Yet being born naïve doesn't mean we must remain so. Our ignorance has served its purpose; the illusions have gotten our attention. Game on. Now the training wheels that first helped us move forward are outgrown and slowing us down. Tears are being needlessly shed, hearts are being needlessly broken; it's time to change our orbit, time *to bring on the dead*. Big brothers and sisters of a sort, though far more intimately than through blood, who yearn to help their tribe and flatten life's learning curve as soon as possible. After all, before long our roles will reverse.

Today, they have what you need: perspective. You have what they need: the world they will soon inherit.

Besides, we're family, they love you, and you love them. And what they have to tell you is absolutely electrifying, transformational, fear killing, and joy inducing—the truth about who *you* are, how *you* got here, and what *you* can do with your time in space.

Of course, the dead don't have the kind of voice you can hear, yet. Nor do they have laptops, keyboards, or Internet access. So, if I may, I'll be your host. I'm as ordinary and extraordinary as you are, except that maybe I remember a bit more. I believe I chose this life, in part, to do just that—remember more—with a mind-set, parents, and other circumstances that have included some fantastic memory enhancers and an inclination to spend 40 of my 53 years blissfully questioning, puzzling, and ultimately tapping into the truth. During those years my main objective has been to live my discoveries: to apply these timeless answers to my life, deliberately shaping it for *my own* happiness and prosperity. For the past 14 years, however, much to my surprise, I've also become a full-time teacher on the nature of reality, living a life that is as much an example of what I teach as it is the cause of my joy. Coincidence? I think not.

I started searching early, as a teenager, and by the time I was a freshman at the University of Florida, my quest for truth led me to dwell upon death—big time. *Why* do we die? *Everyone? Gone forever? Really?!* The next thing I knew, Mom began sending me books[2] that, when combined with my own gut feelings and hunches, answered my questions and rocked my world.

Turns out that wondering about death can teach you a lot about life. The process of opening your mind,

---

2   See Recommended Reading.

while expecting answers, coupled with taking action, knocking on doors and turning over stones, makes you a lightning rod for breakthroughs. Nothing frees you like the truth, and nothing holds you back more than not knowing it. Knowledge is power; it heals what hurts, fills what's empty, clears what's confused, lightens what's heavy, brings friends together, turns dust to gold, and raises the sun. A man or a woman tuned in and turned on to truth becomes an unstoppable *supercoolhappy-lovething*. Yeah, I made that word up. Thanks.

As a teacher of reality, however, I don't make things up. I share what's obvious. I try to make it fun. I have a good time. For instance, over the past 12 years I've been sending out a free daily e-mail called "Notes from the Universe": small drops of truth, sometimes packaged humorously, now received daily by almost 600,000 subscribers. I also write books, record audio programs, shoot DVDs, and host talks all over the world.

By no means have I unraveled all the mysteries of the Universe. I'm still far less aware than my dog or even the grove of cypress trees in my front yard. But I do know the answers to the important questions. I know who we are, why we are, how we got here, and what we need to do to bring about major life changes. Answers *anyone* can tap into—and many have.

Wouldn't you expect, after all, that life and our place in the Universe be knowable? *Really* knowable, including the before and after parts? My experiences, my experiments, my life have shown me they can be. That's what the "ten things" in this book are about: knowing the truth and thereby moving through fear and creating consciously. This is what the dead, along with anyone who is *alive and aware and who cares about you,* ardently want you to know. The parameters for thriving on earth.

When they're not rehashing where they've been or studying what's next, the dead's favored "seat in the house" is in the bleachers cheering you on, not on the couch wiping away your tears. Not metaphorically, but literally. They're watching you, watching humanity, now. Slapping their celestial foreheads, excitedly pounding fists on knees, shouting advice, offering encouragement, whispering sweetness into your ears as you needlessly bumble around in the dark.

> Nothing frees you like the truth, and nothing holds you back more than not knowing it.

In the Clearing

I found the truth and I can help you find it, too. I believe it's absolute, simple, and knowable. Whether or not you ultimately agree with some or all that I share, this book offers insights and perspectives that can help anyone live a happier life—now. It includes a rational approach to understanding what life means and how to live it. You'll see that by first recognizing and then accepting the abundantly obvious (life, miracles, and happiness) at face value, without the usual overinterpretations, justifications, and analysis, you can come to have a more interesting and empowering handle on your fortunes.

This isn't going to be all "woo-woo"! I know debits and credits way better than I know dharmas and crystals. I won't be asking you to weigh everything using your feelings alone. Instead, like the fellow life adventurer I am, as if watching over a sleeping compatriot who's about to miss breakfast, I'm going to nudge you a bit and gently shake your shoulder to help you awaken and see that something incredible is going on. Something absolutely wondrous. And that you are at the center of it all.

That there's an ever-present, yet sometimes imperceptible, benign intelligence that pervades the enormous vastness of reality, from the center of the earth to the farthest reaches of space, yet given the immeasurable scope and seemingly impossible magnificence of *just what we can detect*, it's safe to say that everything has a reason, there have been no mistakes, love makes everything better, and what doesn't make sense yet one day will.

That we ourselves are permeated by this benign intelligence, and given the overwhelming evidence from our own lives so far, we can, to a significant and profound degree, direct it at will.

I found early on in my quest for answers—and this has no doubt occurred in your life—that the longer I dwelled on a question, the more inevitably I received its answer, whether conventionally in a book that "coincidentally" crossed my path or through a mysterious sort of osmosis. That these words have found you is exactly what I mean. But given the hot topics I touch upon herein, that you are no doubt ready to examine from angles never before considered, I'd like to caution that any passage, phrase, or chapter of this book *read without the context offered by the entire book* may be disturbing or even misleading. So I strongly advise that you either read it cover to cover or simply leave it untouched, lying around your home until an avid-reader-friend finally "stumbles" upon it, reads it through, and reports his or her complete findings to you.

Finally, in fairness to the dead, the following chapters surely do not speak for them all. Among the dearly departed, some are certainly more concerned with plotting a hopeless revenge, evading a nonexistent Lucifer, or pleading with a handsome likeness of their favorite prophet than caring about the nature of reality, of which they may know very little. They'll eventually get on board as surely as day follows night, but in the meantime, death doesn't bring automatic enlightenment. It's a regrouping phase for the former living to reconvene, share, laugh, cry, self-assess, strategize, and prepare for what's next. The following chapters are therefore from those "dead" who are "in the know" simply by virtue of experience, the "old souls" who would like to reach those who *want* to be reached—those ready to learn life's truths so they can far more happily get on with living.

Yours in the adventure,

Chapter 1

We're not dead!

It's odd how people like to be told what they already know, as if being told makes it more real. This is why the number-one thing the dead want to tell you is that no one dies. Not ever. Not anyone. Including you. You're going to live forever, gallivanting throughout realities and dimensions unimaginable, carried onward by love, all misdeeds forgiven, infinite possibilities on deck, surrounded by friends and laughter, unicorns and rainbows, celebrated as the god or goddess you are.

Yes, as much as it seriously risks all credibility, you deserve the full truth: if you want unicorns, you get unicorns.

Forms change, shapes shift, energy exchanges, but even the humblest of today's greeting cards has the depth and clarity to remind you of what you already know: those recently departed loved ones are in "a better place." And while you can tease or torture yourself by wondering if this is really true, doesn't every religion echo that life is eternal? Haven't scientists proven that matter is not solid, but *organized* energy? "Organized" being the highly operative, fully loaded, bursting-with-implications descriptor in this case. Don't your nighttime dreams hint at the obvious separation between consciousness and your physical body? And aren't there enough recorded incidences of the paranormal to give even the most diehard skeptics pause?

Yet in spite of this, in spite of a belief in an afterlife and a loving superintelligence, little in the human adventure can be as debilitating as coming face-to-face with the death of a loved one, which to the physical senses means good-bye—*forever*. Even when saying good-bye to the same person just a day before, perhaps as they drove off to work or went to school, you managed an appreciative, nonchalant smile. For death's arrival, however, there's just sheer, total, and absolute devastation.

Only the truth can help you now. Crystal clear, absolute, yes-or-no truth. It exists. More solid and dependable than the Rock of Gibraltar. And while the dead can't instill it within you, they can reveal it to an open mind and offer tools and stepping-stones to help you own it. Through deductive reasoning, connecting a few safe dots from known science, simplifying, extrapolating, and concluding, you will soon sit upon your rightful throne, living in everlasting peace, untroubled by the monster previously known as death. Knowing that every "good-bye" means a new "hello" and that the bigger the former, the grander the latter.

What's Really Going On

Let's first consider the obvious: inanimate objects, like rocks, will never evolve into having personalities, favorite colors, or best friends. Why? Because consciousness is not produced or created by matter. Right? It doesn't happen in laboratories, and in the history of the world it's never happened in nature. Sure, there's consciousness, but to assume it *originated* from, or exists because of, matter has no basis.

So it follows that independence from matter (matter being held and defined by both time and space) would also mean independence of time and space. Meaning that whatever else consciousness might be, it was first a timeless, formless essence. Yes? Easy? Comfy? And this, pretty much without any effort, paints a fairly clear picture: You, the formless and eternal, now temporarily possess a physical body, chemically and organically borrowed from the substances of earth, to channel your nonphysical energy and personality as you negotiate space, travel through time, and experience what has become known as life. Voilà!

"Whoa, fella, way too fast! Besides, why?" you want to interject.

Hold on. We're building a case that will take all ten chapters to present, including *"why."*

So, to play a little devil's advocate: If, as many people today reason, "dead" is *dead*—lights out, all done, forever and ever—wouldn't that mean everything else under the sun, including the sun, is relatively pointless? Stupid even? And if life is essentially pointless, wouldn't the basis of life itself be without intelligence (which is actually what "stupid" means)? And if there's no intelligence, wouldn't this mean life as you know it is pure happenchance? And that your own existence today is unintentional, random, and, if you're having a pretty good time, a mighty stroke of *unimaginably* good luck—statistically crushing the odds necessary to win the lottery every weekend in a row for 10,000 lifetimes?

It would.

Whereas, returning to where we left off, if "dead" is not dead and you therefore carry on transformed, again, wouldn't that positively and absolutely mean that time and space cannot be bedrock reality? That consciousness, originating elsewhere, is similarly free to exist beyond them? Yet as it's present within the illusions, there must be a reason? And for reason to exist there must be order? For order there must be meaning? All evidencing, once again, yet from a new angle, that an intelligence exists independently of time, space, and matter?

Yes, it would.

Keeping at this, gently seeing the obvious without drawing too many conclusions, drilling down to truth, you'll also see how to know much more. And you'll learn that nothing else in all the world is as important to you as understanding exactly what *is* going on. These pages are taking you there.

You **are the reason the sun rises each day, literally.**

OCKHAM'S RAZOR

William of Ockham, or William Ockham, was a 14th-century Franciscan friar, scholar, and theologian from Ockham, a town in Surrey, England. He's famous for absolutely nothing other than being (debatably) credited with devising the simplest of tools to get at the truth of any issue, now known as Ockham's Razor. A razor being an instrument used to remove what is unwanted: in this case, speculation, lies, and fluff. Paraphrasing, it goes something like this:

> Of two or more competing theories, the simpler theory is most likely correct.

Essentially, Bill's saying that to get to the truth of any matter, *keep it simple.* Don't connect too many dots. Don't buy into any premises or go off on any tangents that aren't necessary to have a sense of peace and confidence or that cloud the clarity you achieved with your initial collection of connected dots.

To illustrate, while time and space most certainly contain an *infinite* number of truths—some known, most unknown, each debatable—there's one dot that can be connected for which virtually all people would be in agreement, which provides both peace and confidence, and it is:

Dot 1: Today is a beautiful day.

Yes? Do you agree? If it's pouring rain wherever you now are, please see the good in it. Now of course you could rightly argue that in some quarters, where there's suffering and misery, today is anything but beautiful, but wouldn't such quarters be exceptions? Painful exceptions, yet exceptions nonetheless? Is it not fair to say that taken as a whole, as experienced by the majority of life-forms on this planet, although each life has its challenges, it is still beautiful?

Depending on the time of day wherever you are, it was; it is; it will be.

With this truth about life on earth revealed, does one not now have some degree of traction? Information with which to base decisions, chart courses, and make plans? Knowledge, after all, is power. If today is a beautiful day, as was yesterday and, by deduction, as will be tomorrow, you can choose to enjoy it. Dance life's dance, go out into the world, find friends, seize each moment, spin, twirl, skip, jump . . . oh, the power of connecting a dot.

Okay. Now to see what Ockham was getting at, let's connect some more, *unnecessary*, dots:

Dot 1: *Today is a beautiful day . . .*
Dot 2: *. . . because this is the calm before the storm.*

Hmmm . . . Well, perhaps *it is.* Perhaps not . . . Maybe you should rush to batten down the hatches! On the other hand, since you've never battened down hatches before and you've done just fine, perhaps you can continue on your merry way and hope for the best?

Do you see how by connecting one more *unnecessary* dot, an iffy dot, the legs have been knocked out from under the table and traction's been lost?

Or let's connect a different dot:

Dot 1: *Today is a beautiful day . . .*
Dot 2: *. . . because last night you called Mum and didn't lose your patience, and therefore God is rewarding you with sunshine and warm breezes.*

Huh?! Suddenly *God* is on the scene? Judgment is implied? And, *what?* Others nearby who are enjoying this beautiful day are the unwitting beneficiaries of *your* "good" behavior? What kind of day would they be having if you forgot to call, or worse, *if you lost your patience?!*

Again, by connecting just one more dot, the legs have been knocked out from under the table. Yet—and here's the problem—the philosophical modus operandi of the living today is often that *he or she who connects the most dots is closest to the truth,* or in some circles, *closest to God!* Those who hold to the latter are often terrorists and extremists, based on iffy dots they let other people connect for them.

Letting other people connect your dots means living by other people's rules. With Ockham's Razor and by turning within, you can answer your own questions.

Where You Came From

You're okay with time and space being relative, right? Different from one person to the next, yes? Therefore, more illusionary than solid? Not what they appear to be? Okay?

Dot 1: *Time and space (and therefore matter) are illusionary.*

Well then, if time and space are illusionary like a mirage, mustn't some realm exist that supports or gives rise to the illusions? Something *closer* to a dependable baseline? Like a desert is to a mirage? Not that you have to understand or know much about such a realm—too many dots—but mustn't it exist? Perhaps like a dimension that "precedes" or exists independent of the illusions?

Yes, it must.

Dot 2: *There is a realm where neither time nor space exists.*

So what one thing do you suppose you might find in a realm or dimension that "precedes" time, space, matter, and yourself?

Whoa! Lots and lots and lots and lots of dots, all seemingly unconnectable. It's at this point in our quest for truth that we usually become overwhelmed and give up, letting others arrive at answers. But fear not, because there *is* at least one dot we can connect, just *one,* that won't feel uncomfortable, improbable, or forced.

Awareness. Yes? Some form of awareness, aka intelligence (which you agreed to a few pages ago, as opposed to life being stupid), must have existed pre–time/space/matter. You could call this God if you wanted—it works, same-same—*but please don't,* at least not yet. That's what people normally do without even thinking about it. But because to each person God is a vastly different collection of other dots that represent different beliefs, the collections of dots become completely unrecognizable as you go from person to person.

Dot 3: *In the realm or dimension that "precedes" time, space, matter, and yourself, you'd find "awareness," or call it God (but not yet).*

Yes, these are ridiculously simple observations/dots, yet of the most profound and important nature imaginable. It's crucial that you play along, get on board, and admit the obvious, because *your happiness and the control of your life* hang in the balance. It is perhaps among your greatest responsibilities to understand as much as you can, however simple, about your presence in the cosmos.

Hang on: you're about to blow the lid off of this Popsicle stand.

What else might we call "intelligence," "awareness," or "consciousness"? How about "thought"? Doesn't "thought" generally equate to or make possible all of these?

Dot 4: *Even pre–time and space, you'd find some variety of* thought!

WHO YOU MUST BE

And *mustn't that mean* that if "where" there was once only intelligence, awareness, or *thought*, there now exist planets, mountains, and people (time, space, and matter) . . . *What must planets, mountains, and people be made of?*

Yes! Golden! That's right! They must all be made up of thought! Thought that became "things"!

And, *look who's thinking now* . . .

Okay, we're getting ahead of ourselves.

Dot 5: *Thoughts* became *things. Thoughts* become *things: TBT.*

Obviously, when we say "things" we also mean circumstances and events, which are actually just moving things. Right?

So, thought is the prime mover of all "things" in time and space. Thought: consciousness, intelligence, and awareness. Or call this trio God. But more—fantastically more: if "where" there was once only intelligence, awareness, or thought (again, God) there now exists, among other things, you . . . *who must you be?*

You *must* be *of* that consciousness, intelligence, and awareness, which similarly and indisputably means you must be *of* God, *by* God, *for* God, *pure God yourself.* Literally the eyes and the ears of the Divine come alive within the illusions of time and space, the dream of life.

You simply can't *not* be God; what would you be if not *of* that original awareness? Where would you have come from? What would you be made of? As if there could be non-God! There *is* nothing else. All is God. Pebbles, oceans, black holes, you, and all others. Just as you can't go into the kitchen with corn and tomatoes and return hours later with a chocolate cake, neither can you start an equation with pure awareness-thought-God and suddenly have something that is not some derivation of pure awareness-thought-God.

Dot 6: *You are pure God.*

We've not said much and will not say much more about what God *is.* Let God from this point forward be loosely defined: it is aware, it is intelligent, and it is what you and all "things" came from and still remain.

And sure, if it helps you feel better about drawing such conclusions, God is more than you. Infinitely. Unimaginably. There are zillions more dots, *but you don't have to go there,* and just because there are more dots doesn't mean there could somehow be a cell in your body that isn't pure God. Nor should you even try to connect more dots. Please consider that your motivation in this moment is simply to help the "dead" get you to understand that they are not dead after all. Which you are far more likely to believe once you totally get that their existence, like yours, is not dependent on the illusions that you've come to think are so real.

So, let's sally on, as nothing else will improve your confidence more than continuing to answer some of the questions that have vexed humanity since the year dot (no pun intended).

WHY YOU'RE HERE

This is a pretty big dot. Does it make you nervous? No wonder, given the brainwashing of the ages: being told that you are limited, aging, frail, born of sin, into sin, bound to unavoidably sin for the rest of your life, and that you'll be tested and judged anyway. Huh? Why? To see if you didn't sin? Quite an improbable setup. No win/no win. How about we roll back all of those ideas, leave the door open, and not connect dots that don't need connecting?

So, given your rather easy-to-deduce heritage, being pure God yourself, this pretty much means there's only one explanation for your presence in time and space now. *You chose to be here.* If you are *of* God, *by* God, *pure* God, and if God (awareness, thought) preceded time and space, that means that you, a portion of you, also had to precede time and space.

Well, if some form of you existed, pre–time and space, and you're now here, then what other explanation could there be for your presence and that of others, amid these illusions, except that you all had to choose it? Truth is like that. Logical. Simple. Makes sense. Would it make any sense if you were forced here? Who would force God and how? Would it make any sense that you had no input? Might you have been pushed off a cloud? Did you draw the short straw?

Dot 7: *You chose to be here.*

Interesting how many *do* grasp that they'll exist *beyond* the illusions but have trouble grasping that they existed before them. But if time, like space and matter, is an illusion of your own creation (TBT), you must have! Tricky. Obviously your poor grip on this heretofore is because you lack any memory of your past, prior to becoming who you now are in the illusions. But since when does not remembering something negate its existence? And with the littlest bit of further introspection, connecting dots, suddenly it becomes crystal clear why you don't remember choosing to be here . . . *you didn't want to remember.*

LIGHTS OUT; AMNESIA ON

When you watch a movie matinee at a theater, do you want all the lights on or off?

Off, right?

Why?

To see it better! Not just with your eyes, but with your heart. *You want to feel it better.* You want to be with the actors and actresses in each scene. You want to be chased by your fears and then face them! You want to rise above the odds and prevail! You want to be neck and neck with the heartthrob of your choice. *You want to forget*, momentarily, that "you" even exist, so the "greater you" can be entertained and educated. After all, within an hour or two, when the film ends, you'll be back out in the sun, back to who you were. Except . . . you'll be "more" for the experience of having *forgotten* yourself so you could experience another set of rules, as someone else with different beliefs, with different life props, and among different friends—all contained within the script you watched.

The "first" you, the one who preceded time and space, chose the *illusions* you now live among for the very same reasons you might choose a matinee film: the fun, learning, joy, challenge, and more. Yet as the "first" you forgets that it existed first—that it scripted each scene's possibilities, built each stage, and will live beyond the illusions—suddenly the most profound and exquisite adventure drama unfolds! The point being that the "greater" you came first, before the illusions; you, or an even greater portion of you, actually created them so you (the "second" you) could fleetingly get lost in them. And getting this, you can see that *you* are the reason the sun rises each day, literally. You were not an afterthought—you were the first thought. And you will continue to "be" long after the very last star in the illusionary yet spectacular night sky goes dark.

Dot 8: *You wanted to forget who you were so you could fully be who you are.*

All of which further means, in no uncertain terms, that if you chose to be here, *pre-amnesia* and therefore, quite logically, from the zenith of your brilliance (certainly far exceeding what you now possess—no offense), then not only did you choose to be here, but you chose to be who you now are, exactly as you now are: *this is who you most wanted to be!* From an infinite number of worlds and possibilities, you chose as you did not only from a place of brilliance, but as a consequence of such brilliance, with purpose, meaning, order, and undoubtedly a host of other aims, goals, and objectives, for awesome, gorgeous, beautiful reasons.

> **You chose to be who you now are, exactly as you now are: *this is who you most wanted to be!***

You chose everything about who you now are, right down to the shape of your nose, the freckles on your cheeks, the length of your legs or whether you'd have them, your intellectual or emotional inclinations, your personality traits, and everything else you claim as yours this time. (*Of course* you have other "times"; you're eternal, and your dream world is illusionary. But we'll address this later.) And again, it doesn't matter that you don't necessarily know or sense what any of your ambitions were. Such memory lapses are completely irrelevant. Nor does your amnesia mean you can't acquire a sense of what's going on, as we've just reviewed; nor does it keep you from achieving whatever you came here to achieve, just like "forgetting" yourself doesn't stop you from being entertained and educated at movie matinees.

Dot 9: *You are now who you most wanted to be, and you knew exactly what you were doing.*

THE POINT OF LIFE

So what's the point of life? Again, there are too many dots for anything remotely resembling a complete answer, but you don't have to have all the answers to gain massive traction; you only need a few confidently connected dots. To get there, just look for the obvious—at what *does* happen in the course of virtually every human life—then, full stop. Name what virtually everyone else, no matter their creed or culture, would agree with, and suddenly, just maybe, you'll nail the answer to that age-old question *Why?*:

1. To love

2. To be loved

3. To pursue happiness

Within these there are more reasons: to create, to change, to serve, to learn, to laugh, and so on, and so on, and so on. But to keep this simple, these are three main reasons at the top of everyone's list.

Dot 10: *Love and happiness are why we're here.*

That's it! That's enough! Why would there have to be more? Maybe there is more, maybe much more. But until it bites you on the butt or otherwise appears on the horizon, only connect the obvious, simple, and logical dots you can have confidence in.

By asking the hard questions, turning within, and deducing their simple answers, you can begin to see how you fit into the equation of reality creation. As a Creator yourself.

These ten dots not only offer direction and meaning, they reveal the critical moving parts in the adventure of life: you, or better, *your thoughts*. This is the button to push and the lever to pull when you want more love or more happiness, or to make any kind of difference. In this way you can replace lack with abundance, sickness with health, loneliness with friendships, confusion with clarity, and fear of anything, including your old ideas about death, with confidence.

What Happens When You Die

Well, first of all, you won't. Which is all you really have to know about death and why it's the first thing "dead" people want to tell you. Many of them found this hard to believe themselves at first, gazing upon their own funerals, lingering around their old stomping grounds, stunned and amazed as they gestured and shouted to the friends left behind.

There's an abrupt disconnect, of course, that comes from leaving behind all things time and space and learning to maneuver in the unseen. The nature of this transition depends entirely on the beliefs of the dearly departed at the time of transition, because their beliefs and thoughts carry over to their new environs. Even there, thoughts become things, only they become things bigger and faster, arranged to match the expectations of new arrivals, often in the twinkling of an eye.

Harps, angels, Jesus, Muhammad, Buddha, Krishna, and lots more deities, saints, and whatnot all have energy fragments (not as crude as it sounds) on standby for the constant flow of new arrivals who will be welcomed, scolded, praised, or celebrated in any number of ways *based upon the deceased's anticipated and believed-in scenarios.* Elaborate "sets" can be seen floating in cloud settings, golden gates are "assembled," gardens of Eden are manifested, fiery dens are ignited—whatever. Remember: in illusionary dimensions such as time and space and the afterlife, these "saviors" can be in an unlimited number of "places" at the same "time." Welcoming committees also include, when appropriate, a cadre of deceased loved ones and those whose lives were affected by the deceased's life and choices. They all take on the physical form and age that pleased them the most as they gather to welcome and assure newcomers that they have indeed survived and arrived somewhere wonderful.

Time is not an issue; the party can last "weeks." Space is not an issue; everything seems to exist just for you. Kind of like on earth, if you've noticed. Communication is done mostly through a suddenly remembered form of telepathy, which will feel as natural to you as shaking hands once did. Travel is accomplished by willing yourself to wherever you want to go. Friends are found the same way. Thought connects all, *is* all. You'll also be thrilled to see that you, too, have taken on the physical form from your life that pleased you the most and that all aches and pains have vanished—and you'll quickly learn how to change even further. "Limitless" has a new meaning for the deceased.

Loving guides soon appear, glowing, radiant, and joyful. They orient you and answer your questions. They teach you. Remind you. Love you. Show you. Everything becomes clearer. You remember the hopes and intentions of your recent life and why you chose it. You review play by play all that happened. You see how things lined up or didn't, and why. You're awed by your power, wisdom, and kindness, saddened by what you missed, mistook, and misunderstood, yet inspired to know you can try again, make amends, and move forward with and into even greater love. Past lives come into view, along with the friends, loves, and lessons they contained. Everything starts making sense. It comes together like the most amazing artistic creation, a masterpiece that boggles your mind with its perfection, and you are humbled to find the paintbrush still in your hand.

> **Time is not an issue; the party can last "weeks."**

HELLO, GOD?

There may be a personage representing "God," if you manifested such upon your arrival, given your beliefs and expectations. However, as things become clearer, your need for this disappears, and you are left to contemplate the wonder of existence and the miracle of your mere presence, eventually grasping that God is All, always, everywhere at once, not human but "alive" within you, and that no symbol, shape, or figure could ever come close.

As your sense of acceptance and awe grows, so do your confidence and joy, and the more anxious you become to move into new adventures with those you love and who love you. Options are shown to you and weighed. You can choose to stay as long as you like in this new, more pliable world of illusions, but you can see that you are there only because of your earlier presence in the denser time-and-space jungles and that you have much more to learn. This lighter, more ethereal version of the jungles exists solely as a place to refresh, cleanse, and regroup. Ultimately, all of your experiences within these illusions and those on earth meld into all that you ever hoped to attain: *all that God ever hoped to attain by being you*, at which point pathways for moving beyond the illusions appear. Like what? We don't know . . .

But best of all, perhaps, at least for now, all of this means that your dearly beloveds who've already transitioned did not die. Rather, they're resting, rehabilitating, and "dreaming" in a rather spectacular "place." They're now among friends and guides, and should you permit them, they'll be at your big homecoming celebration, laughing, crying joyfully, teasing you, even as they sometimes do right now, in the unseen and just over your shoulder . . . nice bunny ears.

From a Dearly Departed

Dear Kirsten:

I know this may come as a shock, and you know I'm not fond of using stale one-liners, but "reports of my death have been greatly exaggerated." I'm as "alive" now as I was on the day we met, except, maybe . . . even more so.

Not that this is heaven. I'm not sure if I didn't qualify or what, but I'm not complaining. Here, it's way better than I ever thought heaven might be like, except there's been no Pearly Gate, no appointments with God, and no time to rest!

Yet as quickly as I've come to know my way around, I've become nostalgic for earth. Even though blues are bluer here, maple syrup tastes more maple-y, and we can all converse with the animals, earth has something . . . different. A fleeting quality made possible by the seeming absolute natures of time, space, and matter. A flower on earth seems much more delicate and precious than a flower here.

There's no question that where I am is closer to "home" than anywhere I've ever been or imagined—mine, yours, and everyone's home—but earth takes the lightness of being to an almost unbearable height. Here, love is palpable, comfort abounds, one's identity is unquestionable, perfection is pervasive, and all seems as it should be. On earth, you can only sense these things in a scattered few moments during your entire life.

Still, this isn't home. I can't even say that I remember home or know "where" it is. This place is more like a vacation from the intensity of earth. We all zip around as fast as we can think; it's super cool. I have friends, places to go, things to do, even a car I sometimes wash just for old time's sake. Honestly, though, it's a little boring. I have a soulful yearning to return to the razor's edge of reality creation. I'm being shown that by returning to time and space, learning more, becoming wiser, we'll eventually be ready for an even bigger move, even closer to home, beyond where I now find myself.

Of course, on earth there's fear. No fear here! And on earth, there's that never-ending sense of peril that comes from living by your physical senses: the insecurity, timidity, self-doubt, and bouts of self-loathing. The rampant psychosis of worrying about what others may be thinking of you. Earth is like an exotic school of adventure and learning filled with desire and heartbreak, abundance and lack, feast and famine; the list of extremes, as you well know, is infinite. But that's just it! The dichotomies of time and space make every decision feel like you'll either wind up with all or nothing! Have or have not! Here or there! Now or later! And this ever-present sense of "or" is what unleashes tidal waves of emotion that are so extremely compelling. Emotions that do not exist here!

To top it all off, one of the first things you realize here is how safe you always were on earth, how guided and protected you were, how in charge of your own experience you were, how you could truly make anything you dreamt of happen next—in spite of appearances to the contrary. No wonder everyone here wants to go back. Not that we're unhappy, mind you—Oh! It's 12-moon-30! I almost forgot ... Solar gliding, my new hobby! Hon, will you excuse me? I have flares to catch, and then some studying for my next ...

Yours until the end of time (which really isn't so far away),

Johnny

DON'T WORRY, BE HAPPY

If you knew, really knew, that your past loved ones were just around the corner and you'd see them very soon, wouldn't that change *everything?* Then let it. Rest assured that in the love of the Universe they are now alive, well, and—perhaps surprising to you—very busy. Their wish for you is to be the same on all three counts. They will prepare a seat for you at your homecoming banquet that will be quite unimaginably grand, yet for now there's a much greater celebration at hand: your life. Until then, know there's nothing to fear in death, least of all a devil in hell, which just so happens to be what the dead want to tell you about next.

CHAPTER 2

THERE'S NO SUCH THING AS A DEVIL OR HELL.

There has perhaps been no lie greater than the one told of a devil awaiting sinners in hell. Any good it may have done in preventing people from sinning has surely been offset by the mass manipulation it makes possible, extracting subservience from what become confused, unhappy lives filled with regret, guilt, and fear.

Of course, for sinners discovering the lie while crossing the threshold between worlds, instead of having to meet their maker—or worse, a big red devil—it makes possible a delirium of joy that is quite unrivaled. They are elated to find that not only are they immortal, but they're approved of, appreciated, forgiven, and adored, just exactly as they are. *If only,* they solemnly think to themselves, *I'd known this while living . . . how different things might have been.*

Fortunately, they see clearly that eternity still beckons and happy opportunities abound and maybe, just maybe, they can take what they've discovered and share it with those who are still living.

THE BEGINNING OF FUN

First of all, it's the dichotomy of the illusions, again, that seems to make *everyone* wrong. To you, if there's an up, there must be a down; if there's black, there's white; if "before," then "after." And from where you are, within the illusions, you're right: there are! It's just that the illusions of time, space, and matter *are illusions*. You unknowingly live your life inside a "house of smoke and mirrors" while attempting to explain the world outside. Naturally, given such a handicap—exacerbated mightily by not knowing you're handicapped—there's a general belief that if there's a God, there *must* be the opposite: a devil. Yet things are *so* not as they seem.

What most can't see is that without the illusions, there's no time, no space, and no matter, and therefore no dichotomies.

Which means no here or there. No before or after. No wanting what you have not or having what you don't want. Essentially nowhere to go, no one to go with, nothing to do, and besides, you've nothing to wear. No adventure. No fun. *That's what the illusions are for!*

The price of fun and adventure, as made possible by the illusions, is believing in the li'l ol' "lies" of here versus there, and so on. But once the game is on, it's hard to know where to draw the line, and people take this whole concept to "places" it need not go. For example, it's why some folks needlessly, even when it hurts and terrifies, believe in the devil and hell.

Yin and Yang

Opposites exist within the illusions, which implies something really profound, something obvious that everyone's been missing: *they're theoretical!*

While the dichotomies of time and space can make opposites possible, the truth is they don't necessarily have to exist. They remain as potentials until or unless you create them. To most, however, it's assumed that to have one, you must also have the other. For example, to be happy, you must know sadness; to have light, dark must exist somewhere; to feel cool, you must know hot. Every up means there's a down, and vice versa. Hardly. While the dichotomies create objectivity, with theoretical extremes at either end, it's naïve to think that by knowing, reaching, or otherwise experiencing one end, you must know, reach, or experience the other. Remember, they're all illusions anyway.

There are actually ascetics who shun joy and happiness, thinking it will precipitate eventual depression and sadness. Yet this ignores the fact that love is the glue that holds creation together—not love and hate in equal measure. That life is good, not equal measures of good and bad. It neglects that you are of the Divine, by the Divine, and inclined to succeed, not inclined to succeed and fail equally.

Feeling cold does not mean that later you have to feel hot in equal measure. Nor does living in the northern hemisphere mean that you must one day, inevitably, live in the southern hemisphere. Nor does living a life of joyful service to others mean that the pendulum must swing, turning such good Samaritans into axe murderers. One need not suffer to know joy, nor be afraid that happiness will later require sadness. And neither does a belief in God mean there must be a devil, any more than a belief in heaven means there must be a hell.

It's All Good

All of which kind of evidences the raw goodness of life. Yes, "good" is part of an illusionary dichotomy— nice catch. Still, it's far more accurate to say that life is good than to say it's good and bad. *Which is awesome: it creates hope, gives traction, instills optimism, and fosters cooperation.* It's also far more accurate to say that God is good than to say God is good and bad. In fact, it's as if all the good you have ever heard about life, God, and yourself is correct, but *none* of the bad is. Which leads us to, yes, there *is* a "heaven"—by which we simply mean your awareness continues beyond the grave—but no hell.

Sure, these may sound like airy-fairy, people-serving judgment calls, except there's evidence of their absolute truth *everywhere*. That *you "are,"* that *I "am"*! That *life*, however the heck it "began," *has somehow carried on!* That against all logic and probabilities, and in spite of humanity, it has not run out of gas, imploded, or self-destructed! To the contrary, it continues to expand, get better, and keep rolling!

The commonly believed alternative is that evil exists *on its own,* of its own volition, and that somehow we've just lucked out as "good" keeps gaining the upper hand. Yet if evil existed on its own, wouldn't you think it would learn to be successful, at least in some quarters? That it would get better and better organized and become more and more evil? Has such evidenced itself anywhere in nature? Destruction for destruction's sake?

If evil did exist as a force unto itself, and it became more and more evil, once it crushed and conquered all goodness, then what? Kill itself? Don't you see that if evil existed *on its own*, in any way, small or large, it would eventually self-destruct? It couldn't carry on unsupported; there's nothing to support it. There is only life. It is all good. It's all God. These words are synonymous, absolutes that continue to play themselves out in front of eyes that want to see things as they are:

Life = Good = Love = One = God

While people may long yet do evil and bad things, it is never because they are evil or bad themselves. And while this does *not* seem to be remotely the case in the world today, we've barely scratched the surface of all that the dead want to tell you, much of which will also help you understand the evil and bad things people do.

The Old Argument

"But what if God loved *so dearly* and was so wise, big, and courageous that He gave to His children the greatest gift conceivable: the *freedom* to make their own choices to learn right from wrong?"

Yes! Nice! And with such a gift, all could then live forever and ever and ever, growing and learning and becoming and improving . . . Right? No. Unfortunately, that's not how the story goes. Instead, after some unimaginably brief period, assumed by most to be a single human lifetime, no matter who your parents were or were not, no matter where you were born, when you were born, and no matter how short your life was, upon its termination you could expect that the whole freedom thing was just a test and then would follow judgment and sentencing.

Wait, if God truly loved "*so dearly*" and was truly that magnanimous in handing out the greatest gift, freedom, wouldn't the testing-judging thing mean that somewhere along the way the offer had terminated? How great is your freedom if, hypothetically, during a brutal life on earth—born during a famine, abandoned, sexually abused—you understandably spent the remainder of your life simmering in hatred and doing wicked things yourself, before your murder at age 32? You'd then be locked in hell for *eternity?* Or what if, after a delightful life on earth with loving parents in a modern society, you once cheated on your income taxes and lied to get your child into Harvard, costing an honest child with honest parents that spot? Red-hot pokers forever? Or what if you were the first person in the history of people to never make a mistake or do an unkind thing toward others, yet you accepted no prophet as your savior and rejected all religions? Ashes for lunch, again?

It's a bit counterproductive, contradictory, and arbitrary to give folks freedom to learn and then not only suddenly deny it, but exact a stern punishment *without end.* What if, hypothetically, it took most people a few times "at bat," needing several decades or lifetimes, before they acquired a sense of fairness and justice? Too bad?

What if Soul #19,428,939,045 had failed the first 19 lifetimes and had it not been for the big renege and eternal damnation, on the 20th his goodness would have smacked the ball so far out of the park, with such profound benevolence and kindness for all, it would have permanently altered the course of human evolution, ushering in a golden age of caring and kindness so grand it's not even conceivable on the present plane? Or let's say it might have taken him 19 *million* times at bat before making such a mark in history. If *eternal bliss* lay beyond (mind you, that's a very long time and a whole lot of bliss) for everyone, evermore? Suddenly 19 million times at bat becomes a pittance to pay for such stellar returns. As does 19 billion, or trillion, or zillion, *given the inconceivable scope of eternity.*

The beautiful idea of God "loving humanity" so deeply that He gave us freedom is blown to smithereens on the day such freedom is taken back, considering that on that one day there could have been a breakthrough that now can never be.

And we haven't even posed the greatest of all questions that in a split second, if we even attempt to answer, obliterates the entire notion of hell and the devil:

"Why?!"

Why would such amazing intelligence fumble around with such a pointless drill as having "children" in order to test, judge, and sentence them? The whole notion reeks of the immaturity, boredom, impatience, anger, contempt, sadism, and failure of the age it was crafted in, thousands of years ago at a very dark time in human history. Using this rationale to explain life, can you even think of one dot to connect that you'd have any confidence in? *One reason* divine intelligence would move in such a direction instead of the direction we've deduced where everyone is *of* God, doing their best, learning and growing and improving, forever and ever, in a dream world from which all return, unscathed but more for the adventure, adding to all that God is?

As if God, the brilliance that started it all, that knew how to hang each star in the night's sky and organize energy into matter, wasn't also wise enough to rehabilitate everyone so in need. Big enough to forgive, unasked. Loving enough to refrain from tests, judgments, and sentences. Courageous enough to accept full responsibility for all creation. And great enough to be assured of unblemished success. In fact, the system now in place achieves all this and undoubtedly more, rehabilitating, forgiving, and loving automatically, perfectly dispensing the exact right doses of whatever is called for at the exact right time. It's just that inquiring minds have not inquired enough, or rather, that they've left it for other folks to do—folks with agendas.

TRUTH AS PUNISHMENT

Now imagine, hypothetically, calling your friends in search of someone to join you for a very special concert one month away, only to find every last one of them elusive, noncommittal, and unavailable. Then imagine allowing yourself to grow bitter and resentful, anger mounting, becoming irritable, treating them unkindly in return—only to learn that the reason for their un-availability was your surprise birthday party planned that very weekend. *Ouch!*

Imagine . . . feeling a growing impatience and con-tempt for a favorite co-worker who's become embroiled in bitter office politics, only to discover that the discord arose when your co-worker began defending you from the unkind remarks of others. *Damn!*

Imagine . . . your car being chased by another. A seeming lunatic who's even run a red light to gain ground. You swerve, dart, dodge, curse, worry, and cry, only to find the two of you snarled in traffic many miles from your starting point. And after a few very strange, smiling gestures performed by this no-longer-so-crazed driver, you roll down your window to learn that the only reason for his chase was to tell you that you had left your opened briefcase on the roof of your car. *Dork!*

Imagine . . . choosing a lifetime, in part, to be the guide, the light, and the mentor for someone you deeply love who has far less life experience than yourself. Yet mid-life, *un*aware of your original aim, you study this unusual character you've befriended and begin to notice her unique faults. She's messy, slow, and emotionally un-available . . . you think to yourself that you deserve more from so-called friends! So instead of guiding, lighting, and mentoring, you compare, belittle, and criticize, ultimately losing touch with this acquaintance and foregoing the opportunity you once craved to be of service to someone you deeply loved. *"I am so, so, so sorry!"*

Imagine . . . living in a world of love, where the sun shone daily, animals on every continent played with delight, and every man, woman, and child was motivated by kindness, love, and service. Where opportunity never stopped knocking; you were always in the right place at the right time; and everyone was doing their level best at everything they tried. Where your thoughts would become things, your dreams gave you wings, and everyone was pushed on to greatness every single day of their lives. Yet in spite of all this, at a primitive time in history, the masses, including you, noticed none of this. You were each preoccupied in the dramas of your own circle of family, friends, and enemies who allowed you, even encouraged you, to focus on what was wrong, what didn't work, and what you didn't have. Who told you, in spite of glaringly contradictory evidence, that God was angry, people were mean, and life was unfair; that success was a matter of who you knew, not what you knew . . . Yeah, earth today. *"Do-over?"*

> **Eternity promises too much to spend one more moment looking back with regret than is necessary.**

Every life experience lives forever within you, not locked in your brain but beyond your physical body as part of the very essence of who you are. And it will all be presented again in a final life review, post–homecoming party, after your transition. Everything.

In such a review, you are loved into seeing and understanding not only the motivations and rationales that guided your choices, but the ramifications such choices had for others. You celebrate your triumphs and perseverance, especially as they helped others, and quite obviously you suffer, yet again, through your confusion and misunderstandings, especially as they hurt others. The latter is the closest to hell you will ever come, yet it's not imposed upon you, nor is a devil involved. The only judgment comes from yourself, the sternest judge of all, as you know too well. So you learn and then you move on, closer to the truth in all things, wiser, more loving, and greater than you were before, poised for greatness once again.

Eternity promises too much and people heal too quickly to spend one more moment looking back with regret than is necessary to learn the lesson. Let your guilt teach you, not punish you. And let the guilt of others do the same for them, no matter how grave their misunderstandings.

What about the "Victims"?

And what of the "big stuff"? Like the child who is murdered? The teenager who is raped? The father killed defending his family? Are we now blaming the victim of every tragedy?

As if every answer could be packaged into a tidy little sound bite that would give everyone clarity and confidence and fill them with love. It can't, yet this doesn't mean that specific, meaningful answers don't exist in *every single case*. To reach such answers, however, you need a much wider view of reality and life in the jungles that includes an awareness of your eternal, divine nature and the motivations that may exist behind your incarnational choices. Until we cover everything else the dead want to tell you in this book, please give thought to the following questions that have already been answered:

1. Have we not otherwise deduced that all are gods? Of God, by God, pure God? Student Creators? With eternity still before us?

2. Have we not seen that life within the jungles is illusionary; nothing is as it seems? That it's merely a dimension to visit temporarily for its lessons and adventures?

3. Can anything that happens in the *illusions* detract from their source? Does making monster faces in the mirror make you a monster? Can anything be done to a mirage that detracts from the desert?

4. Don't we already intuitively accept that *every* dark cloud has a silver lining? And that when you see no such lining, perhaps it's because you have more to learn, not because it isn't there?

These offerings neither justify nor make right the hideous and often disgusting violations that occur in time and space; they merely offer a greater context for your consideration. More will be said to bring clarity to this sensitive topic later. The intent now is to help you begin seeing more than what your eyes have afforded.

CANCER HEALS

Cancer, for example, ravages the physical body. Yet instead of exploring it with the immediacy of a microscope, let's stand back and consider it as an *experience* that plays itself out over months or years; we see that in many cases it leads its "victim" into discovering his or her power, appreciating life, or reconciling damaged relationships. Suddenly cancer can be seen in a different light—as an adventure into *healing* one's body, mind, and spirit. With a changed perspective, the gift is revealed: one that was invisible under a microscope.

And while there are many situations that occur in the world that up close are far too horrible for words, we can nevertheless discern that at some greater level there *are* reasons. That a process is unfolding with a beginning, middle, and end; that there is order. And so, however invisible or impossible to imagine in that moment or even in that lifetime, there must also be healing and love. What would the alternative be? That divine intelligence made a mistake? That it was pure chance? That meaningless things happen on this planetary bastion of order, balance, and perfection?

Nothing justifies the ugly in time and space. But by sensing that there are reasons and rhythms, even though they may not yet be known, you can spend more time understanding your creations, living in the present, and shaping your future than giving away your power by dwelling on the past. And in this light, *and only from this perspective,* bad things do not happen in time and space. Everything adds to, and makes greater, the whole.

WHAT ABOUT KARMA?

What do *you* think "karma" might mean? Like the word "God," it gets around.

Essentially, as an *absolute* law, a scorecard, or point system—there's no such thing. If there were, it would interfere with the only principle that governs all manifestations: Thoughts Become Things. If karma were absolute, and once you lied, for example, you had to be lied to . . . well, how could you be lied to unless you'd created circumstances to allow it? What if, after *your* lie, you quickly understood lying's folly and immediately began living at a "higher level," thinking only peaceful, honest, joyful thoughts? Do you see that if by some absolute karmic law, you still nevertheless had to be lied to, it would break TBT! Ain't happening—*no one is limited by karma*. Change your thoughts and you can free yourself from any such "wheel."

Yet sure enough, given that people's underlying worldviews change very slowly, rarely moving spontaneously from liar to saint, it can often *seem* that they live in a tit-for-tat world where their past behavior seems to forecast what they'll experience in the future. Hence the usually accurate cliché "What goes around comes around." For which it is fair to note that karma does indeed appear in our lives, yet more as a phenomenon than as a law.

No one is limited by karma.

To those who understandably yearn for their tormentors to one day know of the pain they've suffered, fear not. So great are the natural mechanics of spiritual evolution, and so great is the desire of the divine to leave no stone unturned toward knowing all things, no one can truly understand their power without *fully* experiencing it from the perspectives of everyone it has ever affected, including their "victims." And because learning your full power is a desired component of every incarnational cycle, they will know your pain in as raw a form as you knew it—whether through "karma" or from a self-cultivated empathy derived from true understanding and reflection.

BEING OF SPIRIT

Religion needs spirituality.

Spirituality does not need religion.

Religion is man-made, time and illusion based, and exclusionary. Its origins were obviously noble and of good intent, as is true of God/Man. It was an attempt to explain the hard-to-explain, recognizing that there's more to life than what the physical senses can perceive and more to science than instruments will ever detect. As it evolved, however, religion drew ever wider and more tangential conclusions, generally led by individuals who wanted to show that they were closer to God than other people—which, as mentioned earlier, was supposedly evidenced by connecting more dots than others did. And the masses, threatened, humiliated, and too overwhelmed with survival, ceded their power.

Eventually, religion began making up dots where no dots had ever existed. And from such connections men fashioned laws, rules, rituals, hierarchies, penalties, rights, and privileges, all for believers (unless they're "bad"), and a total lockout for nonbelievers (even if they're "good"). You either belong or you don't. You will either be saved or you won't. And pretty much anything done in the name of the religion is okay, including lying, dying, and killing.

Spirituality, on the other hand, is usually more of an acknowledgment than an explanation. "In God we trust" is such a sentiment, intentionally connecting the fewest possible dots. It's timeless, needs no illusions, and includes everyone. More, it typically places God within "humanity" (and all things for that matter) rather than apart from Him.

Everyone, *being of spirit,* has the capacity to grasp the folly of their ways and the needless pain they've inflicted upon others; ultimately, doing so is an inescapable part of your passage through the jungles. Perhaps not as quick a passage as those who were violated would like, perhaps not even within the lifetime the violation took place, but there's no escaping the reach of your own divine intelligence, power, and responsibilities, and there's no way home but back the way you came.

And everyone, *being of spirit,* of love, of God, has the ability to know in their heart of hearts that there's no such thing as a devil or hell.

> There's no way home but back the way you came.

From a Dearly Departed

Dear Mom,

I'm sorry. So sorry. I thought of no one but myself. I wanted to take a stand, be a man, and show the world they were messing with the wrong person. I also wanted to hurt you and everyone who cared about me, because I felt that it was your attention and love that made me into such a coward and weakling. I blamed you, not knowing then what I know now.

When I pulled the trigger I expected the shot to be followed by silence, darkness, and, finally, peace. Instead, at first, there was total chaos. Loud sounds, buzzing, machine-like humming, and then an intense light, a swishing, everything moving, flying, and, finally, my blurry vision and jumbled mind gently giving way to warm and welcoming faces, gentle voices. I thought it was a dream or some weird altered state. I felt so much love, it made me think of you. It was so beautiful. I felt so much joy. I didn't even know I had died; in fact, I thought to myself, *OMG, I'm so glad I didn't go through with it.* But I had.

In an instant I understood so much! Things that there are not even words for. And it all made sense. It was so obvious, perfect, and precise! I knew why I had chosen to be me, how we all agreed to be the family we were. I saw our prior connections, our chosen strengths and dispositions, and, above all, how we all knew of the probable futures these choices might create. I could see we all knew the directions we might go, individually and as a family, the opportunities we might create, the challenges and joys we might face. Nothing was predetermined.

Fate has no role in any lifetime, yet it was as if all the likely outcomes were known in advance . . . outcomes in the sense of what feelings and emotions we'd ultimately achieve—like happiness, sadness, peace, resistance, creativity, reflection, and more—but not in how we'd get there or what would happen. That was the variable. The "hows." For the first time in my "life" (yes, I'm still alive), I "get" infinite. I saw how every decision we make creates tangents and possibilities that will bring with them unforeseen forks in the road, and more decisions, and more tangents and possibilities.

I was then shown how else I could have dealt with my life's pain and isolation. Perspectives I could have held, insights I could have gained, decisions I could have made, steps I could have taken. I saw how my challenges complemented your challenges and how we helped each other much more than we thought. Mom, please forgive yourself. I beg you. It was my life and my decision.

It hurts me more than the gun ever could have to see how you have suffered, and to see the meticulously crafted opportunities *I had* that I let slip through my fingers in life. I never knew how close I was, how fast things can change for the better, or how much "magic" there was to count on. I didn't think it mattered, I didn't think I mattered, and I didn't know how deeply my decision would hurt so many. I was so wrong.

How desperately I wish I could undo what I did . . . Yet I'm also comforted by all that I feel here, sufficiently to be excited about planning my return. I'll have another chance and another after that. We all get as many as we need or want. I've also been shown that you, Mom, must go through what you are going through and that your choice to suffer is your choice and can only end when you choose to let it. This fork in the road of your life is a gift that we always knew might present itself if I chose as I did, you knew it wouldn't be easy, but you knew it would most certainly be within you to see things as clearly as I'm now describing them. You knew—we all did—that I might make such a choice. And we all agreed that it would be worth the pain we risked to have the time together that we did.

Because you loved me so much, I was able to make the decisions I made, including my last, and learn as much as I did. There are not enough words to thank you for paying such a steep price in love, all for my own growth and glory. But you don't have to worry about me anymore. I'm fine. I've been lovingly welcomed "home." I'm adored. We all are. You are. All that you and I shared lives with me now in my heart.

Mom, we still have forever. And more adventures await than even I, from here, can imagine.

Breathe. Rest. Dream. You've done so well for yourself. It's time to be happy again.

I love you so much,

Your proud son

IT'S WORKING

You are not alive to be tested, judged, and sentenced. You're alive to live and learn, in unending spirals of love. Everything plays to these greater goals, and every decision you make while living becomes the core study material for your fabulous growth and glory—right down to the time and method of your passing, which is what the dead want to speak on next.

Chapter 3

We were ready.

When the caterpillar awakens as a butterfly, the young sparrow finally leaps from her nest, or the infant gasps its first breath, three things happen:

1. There is relief.

2. There is joy.

3. There is expansion.

And it's plainly obvious, given this trifecta of gains that have come from a prolonged physical struggle, that there ain't no going back, nor would there ever be any desire to do so. And the same is true of the most sublime of all transitions: passing from the physical into the nonphysical, the condition called "death." And while the many stories reported the world over of "near-death experiences" are entirely true, they uniquely involve life adventurers who found themselves in the rather unusual position of having expanded choices that included an *immediate* return to the "living" *as who they recently were*. More often, however, the transitional opportunity, however accidental, bizarre, or forced upon them it may have appeared, was created because they were unequivocally ready to go.

In this chapter, we'll focus on three major areas of inquiry: "why 'you' are here," "when 'you' are ready to go," and a further look at the mechanics of change—how your thoughts become things: all three to reaffirm that the departed knew what they were doing, and to assure you know that now is *not* your time.

THE SCHOOL OF LIFE

The adventure of life is every bit the school of life. The more you learn, the more fun you can have; the more fun you have, the more you can learn.

A lifetime in the jungles can be seen as both an elective course and part of the required curriculum. Required only because you're now moving through a process you chose earlier. This process is made up of any number of incarnations, each offering different experiences, usually measured emotionally. It's the illusions, or your belief in them, that make your emotions possible. All emotions are born of the illusions and are unknown and unknowable without them. To put this in perspective, God, if you will, would not know what it is to feel happy or sad, angry or mad, depressed or alone, shocked or bored, to name just a tiny few, without you. Do you see? You are of God, just a tiny fragment made manifest among God's manifestations in order to revel within them, decide what you like or dislike, and learn how to shape, shift, and move them anew. None of this discovering or exploring would be possible without you and your amnesia. Each life's aim, therefore, is simply *to be,* which means to experience, through feelings, your choices. When you are a young (inexperienced) soul, this will always make you uncomfortable, as your emotions can frequently hurt and cripple, *until* you begin to grasp that you are their source and thus their master.

The initial discomfort in your learning curve was expected and considered in your choice; it was included in the "package deal." It means all is well and you're exactly where you should be, exactly where you chose to be. It does *not* mean something's wrong with you. Nor does discomfort today mean that "life is hard" or that you will always be uncomfortable. You are *not* meant to bear that which you find unpleasant; you are meant to change it. That's why you feel it. Your every twitch of pain and malaise invites you to wake up, pushing you to seek grander truths that will reveal a bigger reality and a more magnificent you, ever closer to an awareness of your true place within reality creation—as a Creator.

> **You are *not* meant to bear that which you find unpleasant; you are meant to change it.**

CREATIONISM VERSUS EVOLUTION

Obviously, if there's an intelligence in the Universe that underlies your very sun, moon, and stars, we're talking creationism. Come on: if there was only evolution and men came from apes, why are there still apes? Further, a purely evolutionary worldview would mean that all life sprang from the amoeba—daisies, insects, tree frogs, giraffes, and you! Yet there's absolutely no trace of skeletal remains to show the gradual evolution from an amoeba to each known species today. Evolutionary skeletal remains show only *tiny* mutations of structure, not complete amoeba-to-elephant mutations. Yet supposedly all these evolved species just happen to get along, fitting into food chains within ecosystems that complement and perpetuate themselves? What a story! Plus, why are there still amoebas?

But equally obvious, as you look at the physical artifacts and skeletal remains that do litter the world, the evolution of each species *also* exists as a tool for refinement and improvement. Creation came first and evolution second, *yet both are still at play in every moment* as illusions are constantly being created, re-created, and projected into space. The mirage in a desert is the same; it's an active, moving apparition dependent upon the desert, its source, at every moment of its existence. Yet in your jungles, the apparitions of time, space, and matter additionally take on properties and follow physical laws, adding to their believability as a reality independent of yourself (more on the need for believability shortly).

More, the physical quarks, molecules, and cells that make up your apparitions are more than a reflective haze; they're *of* God, *pure* God. Sparks of God intelligence, not with personalities yet endowed with traits, characteristics, and attributes. These make up all physical objects, and collectively within each living organism, like an ant, a tree, or a planet, they work as one, *coded* to form the whole, just as the whole is coded to add to the greater mosaic of life as you know it. Unlike in a computer, however, each component itself is "alive" and endowed with its unique brand of intention and purpose, just as is the larger creation it helps to form. Which means that the cells of a monkey all work independent of one another, yet with the intention of making the monkey possible. And the monkey, riding unaware upon its cell consciousness, has its own consciousness, traits, characteristics, intentions, and purposes. As does its troop, as does the species, as does its habitat, as does its planet. Nesting like Russian dolls. Each larger creation becomes more than the sum of its parts yet remains entirely dependent on them.

Therefore, your apparitions are projected, supported, and maintained by God, while at the same time God comes "alive" through them as something even more, in a symphony of creativity. And the cherry on top is . . . you: humanity, and the other species throughout the Universe that are not only alive, but co-Creators of the shared experiences that make possible your private experiences. Limited only by the basic parameters agreed upon long ago by the collective (such as gravity, molecular behavior, and vibrational frequencies) that actually *enable* you to play in your specific jungles while virtually all else remains limitless.

KEEPING PERSPECTIVE

Creationism versus evolution is not an either/or proposition. Human evolution, spiritually speaking, from total amnesia to enlightenment, is a "goal" of sorts and is progressing nicely. But to span the distance you've set out to span means starting as an "infant," alone, scared, and in the "dark," emotionally and physically, accidentally creating and mis-creating until you learn of your power and how to use it. The early learning curve part of the adventure is rocked by disappointments and heartbreak, yet the wisdom acquired later makes possible all that's magnificent and heartwarming, culminating with your own illumination. "Time and space" are *your* university, full of learning in its ideal sense: relief, joy, and expansion; adventure and discovery; friends and laughter; health and harmony. Your life now is but a course. A wonderful course on its own, and one that will make future incarnations even better. And while at times it's utterly confusing and surely unpleasant, such feelings don't mean this life wasn't chosen, or that it isn't serving priceless needs and dreams, or that you don't already have lots to appreciate and enjoy.

If you were to examine the typical life—today, early in your civilization's adventure, out of context, with no idea as to where it's all going, not seeing the harmony, splendor, cooperation, health, discoveries, and achievements that your life and your generation will ultimately help make possible for future generations—you'd rightly conclude that for many, *life in the jungles just isn't worth it!* Such a premature conclusion, though, would be like stopping *The Wizard of Oz* at the point when Dorothy discovers a rusted-out tin man to empathize over his missed life and the opportunities seemingly lost.

SUICIDES

Each lifetime is chosen for *many* reasons, as was the deeper and greater choice to enroll in a series of incarnations within the jungles. Ending a lifetime, physically speaking, doesn't end, can't end, the greater choice of incarnational learning.

Younger souls (not to be confused with young *people*) choosing physical suicides discover this. While they can effectively end the "course" by physically ending their lives, they quickly find they're still on "campus." Just as alive, just as much themselves, only in a post-death version of the illusions—which are now far more elastic but every bit as binding. Again, there's no way out but the way you came; all lies must be outlived, understood, and seen through. And unlike others who naturally complete their incarnations, who become immediately aware of further studies and exciting adventures, suicides must "repeat the course" through a new incarnation to face whatever it was they were trying to avoid. This is keeping with the "plan" *they chose*; this is how they wanted it from the zenith of their brilliance when choosing worlds and dimensions from among infinite possibilities.

Suicides, therefore, never achieve their aim of evading issues, with the rare exceptions of severe, irreversible pain, extreme illness, and the like. Although even these issues would not belong to them by chance, and part of their gift would likely come from facing them, not evading them. At best, issues leading to suicide are temporarily postponed, but the cost in terms of broken promises, shattered survivors, and lost opportunities only compounds the unaddressed challenges.

When It's Not Time to Die

Imagine the jungles as a huge themed attraction: The Jungles of Time and Space. There are different parks within the attraction, each with its own theme and brand of exotic rides, shows, and entertainment scattered about—some scary, some thrilling, some funny, some romantic, some educational, some simple/easy/breezy, and so on, ad infinitum. Each "ride" of the thousands and thousands to choose from is customized for you, on the fly, and is shared with others who seek similar adventures. And each ride generally lasts anywhere from a few moments to perhaps even 100 years, containing innumerable forks in the road, decisions to make, dreams to choose from, lessons to learn, and love.

Get it? The themed attraction is like a planet. Each park is like a different era, nation, culture, or mentality to choose from, and over time, you'll probably choose many rides (lifetimes) within them all.

The choice to enter the attraction is a big one. Gargantuan. It's made only after exhaustive and thorough study and preparation, surrounded and supported by best friends, advised by the wisest of guides, with the clear intention to experience all that the attraction has to offer. You don't have to go; many never do. But if you do, it will be for the grand prize, the full monty, the real deal.

Once "inside," your decision to enter will be followed by many, many smaller decisions, yielding their own fun and learning. When ultimately combined, they will accomplish the overall aim of you eventually experiencing the whole enchilada. The thing is that making the decision to go for the grand prize is made from "outside" time and space. *From that perspective,* you enter and exit the jungles simultaneously. Ain't no thang. Ka-pow, and in the twinkling of an eye you have lived thousands and thousands of lives and are wildly more for it. Yet from the perspective you have during any one of your life-times, consciousness is defined by and dependent upon time and space until you *truly learn* that they're just illusions. Which you can only learn by living *in* them and gaining mastery over them at least to the degree that you're a pretty happy camper.

So consider: one of your Mini-Me's is having a bad hair day, or say, years' worth of bad hair days, and wants off the ride. "Stop! I hate my life! I hate these jungles—they were a stupid idea! I want to die!" So, hypothetically, through suicide you stop your adventure on the "Hairy Mountain" ride. Suddenly, however, you find yourself standing just outside the ride's walls as more people choose to ride it and others get off. Even though you "stopped" *your* ride, the ride itself continues without you, and more, you have not yet evolved enough to move beyond the ride. Nor will you, because such evolution *requires riding the ride,* which was part of the awesome, gargantuan choice "you" first made.

So now what?

With loving guidance—or what you might call coaching—by very experienced riders and trained experts, you decide to take the ride again, or perhaps a very similar one, to learn your way through the confusion you created.

THE TIME TO DIE

A life ends naturally when the adventurer either achieves what he originally came for or when he can no longer achieve it and there are no other alternative, achievable goals. Yet knowing when these criteria are met is almost never conscious, and claiming that you're done almost never means you are. "I got what I came for, there's no need for me to stay, everyone I love has gone, and I am surrounded by idiots." Such comments reveal, very clearly, that there is more to learn.

When a life does end naturally, the "decision" (again, it's not conscious) hinges on probabilities: the probable trajectories of all lives affected by the transition and what will be gained by either staying or leaving. Sometimes it's relevant to also include the probable trajectories of those in the community, state, and world who would be affected by your staying or going—especially for world leaders or world influencers.

As your life unfolds moment by moment, so do your probable futures.

To understand "probable," while all things remain possible and nothing is predetermined or predestined, a much smaller range of probable futures exists, individually and collectively. Probable futures represent what might *likely* happen next based on everyone's evolving thoughts, beliefs, and expectations leading up to that moment. The greater the sense of anticipation and inevitability a future carries for those involved, the greater its chances of being experienced. Free will reigns, but logically, individuals must operate within the collective's massive range of probabilities.

Within that range lie the probabilities of each individual in it. An individual's options, therefore, might be limited by the group's, *although:*

1. If an individual has a great enough vision, it can sometimes change that of the group.

2. No matter what limitations the collective imposes, the individual's choices and possibilities to find happiness and fulfillment remain *infinite*.

3. All individuals know full well about the group they're choosing to be part of, and they'd only ever choose to "play along" (being born into those times) if there were *extremely compelling reasons* to do so in spite of any limitations.

The opportunities that likely exist, given the probabilities created by parents and the time of birth as well as the probabilities of the greater collective, lead to the choice of a lifetime. And as your life unfolds moment by moment, so do your probable futures and the chances to achieve what you set out to achieve. Naturally, as you grow, so do your ambitions, and as you achieve old objectives, new ones emerge. And these likely trajectories, to the degree they can be foreseen, are also considered and weighed before you choose a lifetime.

In some lifetimes, far more is achieved than was originally intended. In others, due to changes in the collective—locally or at large—or within the mind of the one whose life it is, important probabilities can suddenly disappear. And it's the state of such probabilities, present, near, and far, as a function of intended lifetime objectives that determines the time to die.

CREATING YOUR WORLD

To the naked eye death appears random. To the spiritually inclined it appears ordained. Each perspective, however, removes consent from the equation, and self-determination seems entirely out of the question. Yet consent, free will, and choice exist—this is your gig, remember? So the questions become these: How does one simultaneously live under the cloak of amnesia and remain in control? Experience the darkness while holding the light? Live to the fullest while choosing when it's time to "die"?

The challenge with these questions, however appropriate they may seem, is that they're rooted in presumptions created by the divine dichotomy: That you either know *or* don't know. That there is either darkness *or* light. That living can't include dying—as if dying weren't an achievement in every life.

Here's the deal. Imagine, as God, that you wish to forget who you are, to discover it anew. Why? Because you can, or because it's fun, or whatever—it doesn't matter right now. Remember: don't connect too many dots, just the fewest possible to start making some sense of things; the simplest choices are usually the most correct. Well, in order to forget who you are, you need to place yourself "outside" of creation, even though you *are* creation, so that once there you can gaze upon yourself and not know it's you!

To achieve this, the following must be true of your new "home":

1. It needs to appear seamless, complete, and believable, independent of you. (Even though it's entirely dependent upon you. Remember: it's you.)
   The physical universe is immeasurably vast and totally hooked up with all kinds of physical laws and properties—check!

2. It needs to be alive, on automatic pilot, sufficient unto itself.
   Amoebas, living oceans, photosynthesis, plate tectonics—check!

3. It needs to include you, even though you remain seemingly and convincingly apart from it.
   Physical body—check!

4. You must retain some deeper, underlying creative connection to it to achieve your objective, which, remember, is to rediscover and expand your magnificence.
   Metaphysical laws of nature (governing the connection between the seen and the unseen, and between the Creator—you—and your creation)—check!

Following the metaphysical laws, to create anything in the physical world it must first exist in the unseen, in thought: *your thoughts*. Your thoughts will then "become" the things, circumstances, and events of your life. As pointed out earlier, they don't do this spontaneously— that would completely shatter and nullify the physical laws that otherwise keep things working orderly—but gradually. Slowly. Progressively. Mostly in concert with the physical laws.

Instead of spontaneous manifestations, like a gold coin suddenly appearing in the palm of your hand, you draw unto yourself a gold coin that already existed elsewhere. One that will be placed into your hand by a merchant, client, acquaintance, benefactor, heiress, child, parent, partner, or friend, whoever was most readily available, given your life with its probabilities and trajectories and theirs. Wishing for a gold coin and holding its image in your mind sets into motion an absolute symphony of events involving a cadre of people, choreographed with a mind-boggling precision that can only be appreciated, much less seen, *after the fact,* after the process that will draw one to you is complete. Hence, the "law of attraction."

How Thoughts Become Things

This process that holds intact the believability of your reality, while completely transforming it to mirror what you are energetically feeding it, is what "you," God, set into motion in order to have the platform for your dramatic and emotional self-discovery. This process is how each moment of your life is revealed to you. Your life is your projection following these laws to achieve your purposes.

While it may be overwhelming at first, doesn't this make more sense than "God works in mysterious ways"? Of course the logistics are incomprehensible to the tiny human brain. To perform such choreography means that all planetary events and circumstances must be orchestrated behind the curtains of time and space, in the unseen, considering all of the thoughts, objectives, and desires held by more than 7 billion people, which will then be funneled onto a presumed single time line where each person gets the closest equivalent to what they've been feeling, made "real," and the numbers are crunched anew as each second of every day is revealed.

You can't make this sh!t up.

Nor can you get much closer than this to intellectually grasping the true mechanics of manifestation. But *you can* see the evidence in your life as you begin to notice the seemingly uncanny resemblance between your worldview and what physically occurs, paying special attention to which comes first. And just as you might not know how a TV works or what happens when you press the remote button to change a channel, you can still know that it works and that you are the one giving the commands.

When you hold a vision in thought—tangible or intangible, cars or confidence—circumstances gradually realign, players and partners are assembled or scattered, and it's drawn into your experience. *As if* by magic, except that it's by universal law, this is how thoughts become things.

It's the confluence of all this—all that you think, believe, and expect—that shapes your life *and death*. And just as a gold coin might lie on your horizon, so can and does all else you dwell upon, including new relationships, promotions, relocations, adventures, and more. Some of these will appear quicker than others, some won't show up at all, and then there'll be some surprises the logistics and choreography of which are far too complicated for the human mind to track—but not for divine mind.

> **Thinking the loss of a loved one was unfortunate, ill timed, sad, or an accident is to miss the gift.**

And so, just as you will have *no mortal knowledge* of when a dreamed-of gold coin might arrive, the same is true of death. Yet when it does arrive, no matter how it does, it won't be random and it will have been created by the one who moves beyond, because she was ready, the time was right, and the choreography was divinely managed.

SURVIVORS

All such gyrations, attractions, and manifestations, of course, take into account the survivors: loved ones and witnesses. It's obviously not in the way survivors would ever consciously choose, but anyone who experiences the loss of a loved one is similarly ready. There are no accidents. It is seen as a probability that will be worth everything else that has come from the relationship. It's better to have loved and "lost" than not to have loved—especially when nothing is really lost. The loved one's passing wasn't set in stone, but it was within a range of probabilities. It may have hurt like "hell" and been among the least desired outcomes for those grieving, yet they, too, *were* ready:

- ☀ To live life on new terms,

- ☀ To raise the bar on understanding life's "mysteries,"

- ☀ To see through the illusions, and

- ☀ To know that life is indeed beautiful, orderly, and full of love.

Thinking that the loss of a loved one was unfortunate, ill timed, sad, or an accident is to miss the gift and remain in the dark. It denies the perfection and order that are otherwise so abundantly obvious in every life—including its end.

From a Dearly Departed

Hi, Daddy!!

It's Kaley!!! I'm fine!! I'm here!! I love you!!

Sorry about your car. ☹ I know it's me you miss, but still, very uncool about the train ... LOL

Daddy, you told me everything happens for a reason, right? Well, I can't explain the train, but I can explain ... this ... me, here.

Daddy, I got what I came for, to know I'm loved just as I am, that I never needed to justify my existence—you gave me that ... Mom needed the grounding that only a believed-in loss can give ... and you ... if I hadn't died, you would have.

I know you'd have traded places with me, but that's not how it works. Nothing would have been gained.

You've been praying . . . haven't you? A lot. Every day.

You never prayed before, ever. Did you? You once said God was "wishful thinking."

But your prayers have been heard! You're reading this, aren't you?!

Daddy, you're "waking up" to new ideas that until my death you never would have considered. As far as you were concerned, they didn't matter. You made me the only thing that mattered in your life and you stopped living your own. Now, because of the pain, you're looking for proof that I survived because the alternative hurts too much. My passing has done this for you. You talk to God now.

Listen! God is talking back!

As your thinking expands, you'll start to get that my passing wasn't just for you, or for Mom, but mostly, it was for me. You'll see that I got what I wanted—even more, given how much you loved me. You'll get that I didn't really die. That I'm well, I'm happy—there were no mistakes. Don't question, don't even try to understand. It'll make sense for you in time, the way it has for me.

You're starting to consider life's spiritual side, and this will finally lead you to contemplating *your* spiritual side. This means everything, and while the grief feels like it might kill you, it'll pass and you will live like you have never lived before. If I had stayed, none of this would have happened, and you would have died from the boredom, depression, and . . . ultimately . . . resentment when I couldn't love you back in the same way.

You and Mom still have your lives ahead of you. We'll always have all we ever shared in memories—which come back to life here in ways I can't explain—and best of all, we have forever. That's what I most want you to know. It may now seem hard to understand, but of all the new perspectives I have, I want you to know that we will see each other again.

"I love you more,"

Your Little Honey-Bunny

TRUST, FAITH, AND PATIENCE

A crowning achievement and manifestation of every lifetime is one's time and method of passing, yet its probability, like all earthly creations, takes into account more variables than a human mind was meant to handle. Contrary to what your physical senses show you, every death is the product of great order, healing, love, and myriad other considerations that are cleverly orchestrated by the highest intelligence within you. And while these truths can be grossly distorted and misrepresented, it's still worth sharing with those who will understand it, perhaps with the safeguard added: "If you're still living, you're not ready"—which is the next "thing" the dead want to tell you.

Chapter 4

You're not ready.

Being dead may be cool, but cooler still is to be alive in the jungles of time and space—which is why you are.

You came from "dead" and back to dead you'll return, and on the whole, you'll spend far more time "there" than "here." Yet while "there," your main focus will be to hone and perfect the art of getting "into body" (as opposed to your celebrated "out-of-body" experiences).

And now, as you read these words, for just a little while longer it's still your turn on stage. Yet because all this may be challenging for you to believe, perhaps you're skeptical. Maybe you're unconvinced that today is packed with meaning and that you are who and where you most wanted to be. That you're the magician of your life, master of the illusions that dance around you, and an intergalactic tidal wave of love and pure energy. After all, sometimes finding a parking space seems to be asking for too much, while losing weight, paying off debt, and finding Mr. Right can sometimes seem like a cruel joke. No wonder the living love to lament, "I plan, God laughs."

And why *wouldn't* you be ready to die right now? Especially if you're suffering over the "loss" of a loved one? Especially when everything seems so random and chaotic? Especially with the load of "issues" every life seems to accumulate? Especially if you keep getting stuck, don't get what you want, and find that this whole ordeal asks a bit too much of you? This chapter is for you.

Catch-22

First, understand that life within the jungles puts you on the cutting *edge* of reality creation. Little else could compare to the choice of forgetting all in an adventure

that gives new eyes to God, as well as new ears, new feelings, and a new heart that will never cease beating, for
"to be" is "to be" always.

To accomplish this, you're on a journey of your own
creation, yet where you're truly going is *not known or
knowable*. Not even "God" knows, otherwise there'd be
no point in going.

You are here as God to find this out, to blaze a new
trail. You are a pioneer into consciousness—although
looking at life from your mortal perspective, *you
are assured of nothing*. There are angels who dare not
tread where you've trod and who find your courage
utterly breathtaking.

And therein lies the catch of living a lifetime within
the jungles of time and space:

> Life's adventures are only possible because of life's chal-
> lenges.

Not that every high must have an equal low; we already covered that. But that every moment must carry
with it an "or." The greater the "or" you create, the more
thrilling. For example, of all the joys on earth, few compare to the crowning glory of achieving *against the odds,*
succeeding *in the face of peril,* triumphing *over adversity,*
or finding love *where there seemed to be none.* Yet in every
such case, the poor odds, peril, adversity, and loneliness
must come first! Turning 2 million dollars into 100 million is *nothing* compared to turning zero dollars into 1
million, because to do so you must start with . . . *zero.*

Yet these very challenges, these invitations to greatness and pathways to joy, are all too often seen by "the
locals" as problems, curses, and demons! Reason to with-
er and withdraw your magnificence rather than engage

it and turn it up. The whole point is missed. Your life isn't great *except* that you have chicken pox, you're broke, or your girlfriend cheated on you; *your life totally rocks because* you have chicken pox, you're broke, or your girlfriend cheated on you! Your issues aren't random, they're by design. Divine design—*yours*.

> **Life is not meant to be hard so that you can be happy beyond it.**

The dead, therefore, want you to get that no matter where you are, everything is okay, getting better, and happening just as it "should," in a steady progression that will forever take you higher. This is God's trajectory within time and space: eternal expansion. They want you to know that even in their absence, however much you might miss them, the fact *that you still live* is exquisitely meaningful. It means that you still have places to go, friends to meet, and lessons to learn; that there can still be more smiles than frowns, more laughter than crying, and more joy than sadness, in a living, loving Universe that's literally conspiring on your behalf.

They want to remind you that the world is still your oyster, though your "work" is not done. Let go of the past, return to the here and now, and begin shaping the rest of your life. Hang in there and keep dancing life's dance, knowing that you are inclined to succeed and prone to joy because these are propensities of the Divine, traits of the Immortal, your eternal birthrights.

HAPPY ENDINGS

Come on. Would loving parents ever give their child a book to read that didn't have a happy ending? No.

But they might well advise, "Don't stop reading during the scary parts!" And neither would a "greater you" give yourself the gift of time and space if it wouldn't be all good *in the long run,* no matter how things may appear midway. So good that *no matter what might happen,* it would be worth every bump and turn along the way.

As I hope you might suspect, the "happy ending" in this metaphor most certainly isn't when you "die." Life is not meant to be hard so that you can be happy beyond it. The happy "ending," therefore, comes with finally understanding those tricky areas you move through *while* you are alive. The key is that you do indeed need to *move through them* and not "stop reading at the scary parts"; you must prevail, hang on, and keep trucking to emerge on the other side of whatever the tricky area was.

When you have mastered it, a new dream appears from which another journey begins.

Most people trying to understand life, God, and purpose immediately ask about the world's pain and suffering. They never ask:

* ☀ Why do so many people on the planet, from the arctic to the Sahara, have enough food?

* ☀ Why do so many people seem to live charmed lives, with friends, partners, and children?

* ☀ Why are there so many lottery winners, rock stars, and multimillionaires?

But if you want to ask about "happy endings" for children starving in faraway countries, or the horrific abuse that happens in virtually every nation (both very fair and highly responsible questions), you'll have to put them in the context of 7 billion other lifetimes happening at the same time and admit that such tragedies are comparatively few. And granted, even while the number of people who experience some form of violation in their lives is not small at all, those violations alone do not necessarily define those lives, which often are otherwise happy before or after the violations. To judge your life or anyone else's, your progress or the seeming lack thereof, by any spot along the path takes whatever's happening in that moment completely out of context.

Fleeting Glitches; Lasting Gifts

Losses within the jungles are not only temporary but, like time and space themselves, illusionary. What better way to learn this than by choosing a path with probabilities that contain "losses," where misunderstandings can be revealed and then dispelled? Imagine the intoxicating euphoria the bereaved and seemingly abandoned soul feels upon discovering the truth that not only does the beloved live on, but they will be together again, forever. By accepting or even welcoming your challenges, you create opportunities for their gifts to be revealed. Then you're free to revel in the wonder of it all and move boldly ahead on a path that can now take you even higher into the light on even greater adventures than your earlier limitations would have allowed.

Nothing is by chance. To be alive means you knew what you were getting into and knew of all the probabilities that might one day present themselves. Any seeming hole in your life now is a custom-tailored invitation from yourself to yourself to be led to greater truths about life, love, and reality than you would have otherwise ever taken the time to consider. When shaken by a loss or tragedy, a flaw or imperfection, you have the choice to be taken down or lifted up by it. And given the resilience of the human spirit and every individual's innate inclination to succeed, the uplift, eventually, will be your choice. You'll discover that you've remained complete in spite of your challenges, setbacks, and heartbreaks—even that you've been made more by them.

Case in Point: Spousal Abuse

This is a sensitive subject, so to be very clear, nothing justifies abuse of any kind, ever. It is wrong, undeserved, and criminal. Those who commit such offenses should be sternly dealt with. Those who suffer from them should be afforded swift compassion and rehabilitation. Nevertheless, it happens, and because you deserve the hard questions answered, this issue can help illustrate some of the points in this chapter.

So, hypothetically, if a "victim" concluded that she was dying, life was unfair, and her situation had no redeeming hope, she'd be right *in that moment.* If those were her only conclusions, however, she would be seeing the abuse out of context, a context that would include her past and future. Further, if she were then to base major life decisions solely upon these short-sighted conclusions—canceling future plans, avoiding her friends, or allowing anger to build—she'd end up blinding herself to the miracles that surround her, short-circuiting her own healing abilities and concealing the life-balancing and spirit-enhancing insights the crisis reveals. Such as:

- ☀ Understanding that one's worthiness need not be earned.

- ☀ Learning that hearing or saying no is neither a denial of love nor inappropriately selfish.

- ☀ Realizing that it's no one's job or responsibility to save or redeem another.

- ☀ Considering that there's no such thing as a one-and-only "soul mate."

- ☀ Discovering that self-love needs to come before loving others.

- ☀ Finding that being happy and living in peace does not require sadness and violence.

Or literally an infinite number of other lessons and insights, as no two abusive relationships are exactly the same.

Similarly, *all* losses and suffering, illness and disease, disappointments and heartache, lives and deaths experienced within the jungles are of each adventurer's creation. They offer customized opportunities for self-correction, balance, healing, growth, and absolute gain. The long-term (we're talking eternal!) potential good always wildly exceeds short-term setbacks and suffering. When difficult situations are considered over time instead of simply as isolated, random incidents, their hidden gifts become apparent.

Yet there can be little healing, balance, or improvement if the pendulum isn't allowed to swing *or a life isn't allowed to be played out.* Wherever you are right now, it's right; it's where you're supposed to be. Not because it's destiny, but because of the choices you've made and the focuses you've chosen so far. And while there will be times when where you are feels uncomfortable or unpleasant, the trail you're now on is inevitably leading you to more friends, more love, and more enlightenment. It is leading away from confusion and misunderstandings and toward clarity as you learn through trial and error of your profound power over every illusion in your life.

THE PLOT THICKENS

Knowing that no one ever just randomly finds him- or herself in threatening or difficult situations is perhaps the first step in realizing that you are not vulnerable. The first step in knowing that life need not be seen as a scary place that sometimes randomly throws daggers at you. Everything that happens is "written in" by earlier thoughts, beliefs, and expectations—intentionally or, more commonly, unintentionally. The latter isn't so much fun except that for this very reason (not being fun), people will eventually begin asking new questions, correcting old ways, and deliberately blazing new trails.

In the meantime, by understanding how everything comes together, you will more easily find meaning and acquire the inspiration to press on.

The story of every life unfolds in much the same way as the plot of a novel or Hollywood movie: everything with a purpose—vital, planned, and weighed—and with nary an unnecessary character. Not predetermined or random, but written spontaneously from behind the scenes in the writer's lair, which is purposely hidden from view so you can fully experience each twist and turn.

Please don't confuse random with spontaneous. Spontaneous rocks. It emerges from a field of probabilities that you control, maintaining choice and meaning. It involves instinct and urge, hunches and feelings, imagination and belief. Random implies the opposite. Empty and pointless. Maybe or maybe not. Chance and luck.

Lights, Camera, Action

Are there any random close calls, near misses, or "almosts" in a movie? Are there characters who almost get hurt, who almost fall in love, or who almost die? Of course not: it's all scripted ahead of time. Characters are cast in advance. Decisions are made, remade, and made again. Narratives are born, edited, inserted. Dialogues crafted, rehearsed, performed. Nothing is left to chance—too risky, too wasteful. Although it sure seems as if there's "chance" when you're watching it from the comfort of your cinema recliner *because it's supposed to seem this way*; only then does it become believable! Nothing else is more important to the cinematic presentation than maintaining the *appearance* of chance. Without an authentic appearance, including surprises, free will, and infinite possibilities, there'd be no emotional value and the production would be worthless. Like one's life, eh?

Time is an illusion. So is space. But they create the "silver screen" for the reality you're now directing. Everything first happens off screen in thought, imagination, behind the curtains, outside of time and space. Where massive logistical planning and coordination can take place in the twinkling of an eye. Where scripts are perfected and executed in the moment they occur, like lightning following the path of least resistance, no matter how shocking or mind-boggling an occurrence or performance. Not even the stray passerby, the distant barking dog, or the fire truck that goes screaming by exists accidentally without reason, design, choreography, casting, and more. And no one gets hurt, falls in love, lives, or almost "dies" without meaning and intelligence. There are no close calls, near misses, or almosts in life, no matter how close or near they seem.

Even the person who is the sole survivor of a plane crash in "real life" comes no closer to death than the person eating French toast surrounded by a loving family on Saturday morning. Not because of fate or destiny—neither exists—but because this is what they've "written." Past and present thoughts and expectations summon the most probable available realities for them to experience, as divine intelligence weaves their scripts into those of 7 billion others, moment after moment, scene after scene.

See where this is going? Do you see that everything in the jungles is a *work in progress,* including your life, including your life today? And that even if you're bored, scared, or feel like quitting, the fact that you still "are" is indisputable evidence that you're not ready to leave the stage?

The Unknown Author

In spite of the mysterious props and moving sets, *which you need not wrap your head around,* you can always sense that everything is playing to the overall good of the story. You can sense this now about your life adventure, no matter what has happened so far. And you can get that when things appear that you do not like or want, change must begin with you, the unknown author who writes with pen marks of thought, belief, and expectation.

Divine intelligence is your responsive choreographer, formulating steps and routines in the form of life experiences that will bring about the vision you hold on to. Crafting experiences that, as they unfold, will seem to have absolutely no rhyme or reason, although in hindsight the perfection will be obvious and the meaning understood.

Your life story's title could be the name you go by and your genre could be the strengths and interests you've developed over lifetimes, and as the star, you're emotionally living out the main character's role as you unknowingly create it so convincingly that you think you're "real." And your most avid reader is "God," who's following every word through the window of your soul.

Now of course you *are real*, just not in the way you think. And none of this analogy is intended to marginalize the human experience. To the contrary, it can be used to discern the truth and then help you revel in the glory of being at one with the Divine. Understanding that it was God's sheer brilliance that dreamed of being Itself *through you, as you*. And thereby you can set out to live on purpose, joyfully shaping the world around you as you master the skills of imagination, patience, and manifestation.

CREATIVE WRITING 101

Every good author has a trick, a great and mighty trick. She can choose to take the reader down a dark and spooky path that's shrouded in mystery and suspense . . . while writing from the comfort of her den, with all the lights on and TV blaring in another room in which happy kids, furry pets, and a loving spouse also reside. The author gets to *make stuff up,* tosses in red herrings, leaves keys in hiding places, puts the villain on a beeline toward the quicksand, and, "coincidentally," had earlier tossed the hero a hat simply to keep him warm, from which he'll later "pull the rabbit" just before the bridge blows up . . . wow! The author has time on her side, or better, creates the story *outside* of time. It's the reader who will experience the story in a logical, sequential order, as it's being read on a time line. The author can go back to the beginning of the story after it's essentially already been completed and add a new character, Colonel Mustered, who will solve some problem that only became apparent upon completion of the first draft! Yet the author is so masterful in shaping her narrative that the reader feels it's spontaneously, naturally, and logically coming to life in the moment the words are read, which, of course, is long after the final draft was written, printed, and bound.

All of this is possible because the author thoroughly understands her role in the creation and accordingly pushes the right buttons at the right time for the results she wants the reader to find in the finished work.

Similarly, the author of a lifetime, who thoroughly understands her role in the creation, *gives serendipity its marching orders* based on whatever "is written" in thought, belief, and expectation for the results she wants in each finished manifestation. This is *your* great trick. Knowing you are not dependent, in any way, on the world around you. It does not have to be played off of, worked, or manipulated to bring about change. In fact, it's futile to try to bring about meaningful life changes by manipulating life's illusions of time, space, and matter. Instead, change their source! Go within to your thoughts and imagination. Envision, and thereby create, new possibilities to which the Universe will respond in the physical world, rearranging your life's illusions.

Your part is the easy part. The Universe does all the rest.

From outside of time and space, using your imagination, you get to dream up what you want to see happen, where you want to go, who you want to be, and what you want to have. As if by magic, details will be calculated for you. The props and players on your life's stage will shift around, rearranged through seeming accidents and coincidences, summoning the right folks and excusing the wrong ones at just the right time, for just the right reasons, in the most surprising yet plausible ways to take you, the star, from where you are to where you dream of being.

Your part is the easy part. The Universe does all the rest. You just have two things to do:

Step 1: Define what you want, and

Step 2: Show up to receive it.

You nail these (instructions to do so are in Chapter 6), and all else will be delivered to you upon a metaphorical silver platter.

As Good as It Gets

With such realizations, given that your life is a gigantic work in progress and that no isolated thought or experience is the be-all and end-all of it, you see that no matter how you may feel in any moment, or throughout any series of moments, you cannot know when you will be ready to naturally "die" until after you have. And no amount of claiming otherwise—no matter how great the emotional pain or how sad the claimant—will make it so, any more than a child closing his eyes makes himself disappear. There's a magnificent production at hand in which you are the author, star, and audience, and the pages are still turning as angels peer over your shoulder to read the story, and even God is on the edge of Her seat. And though you can't see it, you are now in the midst of an upward spiral, higher than you have ever been before in all of your other lives, and still going higher.

So get on with it. *Being patient does not mean being passive.* Move toward your dreams while you celebrate all that does work, all that you do have, and who you now are. Be with friends. Spend time alone. Don't worry. Be happy. Look forward. This is surely easier said than done, but that's just it: if these things were easy, they'd have been done and what would be the point? You signed up for the intensive program: harder in the beginning, more fun thereafter.

Being patient does not mean being passive.

There's nothing wrong with your life because sometimes you feel lost or incomplete; this means you're "normal," growing, and exactly where you "should be" and all is well. You're not handicapped by your challenges and desires but blessed by them, even if they include missing a dearly beloved who was "ready" before you ... *you are blessed especially when you miss such a person, for the love you knew and still know.* The greater the perceived lack in your life, the greater the dissatisfaction, *the greater the comeback and future celebration.*

Don't bother thinking or wondering if it's "your time." It's not. You'll know soon enough.

And by the way, you're going to miss earth. Everyone does.

From a Dearly Departed

Alexa!!!

WOW, what a flight! I mean ... what a crash! Crazy!

Who dies in a plane crash, right? Almost no one. "It's the safest form of travel, blah-blah-blah," except ... well, yeah, I totally beat the odds.

Dude, I'm alive! The only thing different is that I can hear and see you, but you can't hear and see me. The floaters said I was ready and that you weren't. Yeah, they float around like ghosts, but they're so loving and wise you want to cry. They said I'm now a floater, too, but I still have legs ... here at least.

No ... I can't see you when you take a shower. Seriously? There's like an automatic barrier-thing that keeps anything you want private to remain private, so long as it's not part of someone else's adventure. Like you kissing Bob when he was still my boyfriend, before the crash. That was part of my life. I saw everything in the debriefing after I arrived here. E-v-e-r-y-t-h-i-n-g, "Lexie!"... But if you're kissing him now, I won't know because it's not part of my life anymore.

"Tramp!" LOL, just kidding! It's impossible to stay mad here—there's too much to be happy about. Besides, I already knew, and it's not as if I was a saint. Sorry, you'll learn about that in your life review . . .

Man, the stuff you find out here!

Hey, did you ever notice that I wasn't too friendly with our humanities teacher at school, Mr. Gresham? Guess what! He was my father in a past life and he left my mother and me in the woods, all alone, after I was born. We died of hunger and cold. Creep! Believe it or not, everyone living, deep down, has a sense of their prior wrongs and they usually try to make amends in future lives without even understanding exactly why. Yeah, remember I got an A in humanities? I think it'll take a little more than an A for murder! Well, I don't think that's the whole story, but I was glad for the A.

Lexie, I mention this because . . . I have something to confess. I once hurt you, like really badly. As in, knife attack. Really. Sorry. We were druids, living where Galway is; Bob was there, too—I should have knifed him instead, LOL! No, not really! Knifing has huge sucky consequences. Anyhow, sometimes friends like to return together to work things out or just because they like the same kind of adventures. I'm really sorry. You forgive me now because you forget, but oh, crap, when you get back your memory will be on again.

Hey, something else cool. Because I already knew you were kissing Bob and I let it, and him, go without a fight—no resistance, didn't even tell you—it meant I was free from something that had always held me back. I was able to let him go because I had finally learned that my happiness didn't depend on someone else and that no one's lies can make me less happy. I got what I had most wanted. Those were my lessons . . . plus I learned sharing as a kid—a bigger deal than it seems. Kind of the same. But that's why I died, or at least came here. Cool, huh?! Told you. You should see where I'm going next, except I can't tell you . . .

Anyway, what a flight! Glad you're okay! Please know that I am, too! That you survived, "Lexie," just means you still have more adventures there. That I "died" just means my next adventures are elsewhere. But we can keep meeting like this, and like we do when you dream at night, even though you don't remember those, and like we will forever and ever, here and there and everywhere.

I love you, Sis! XOXOXOXOXO

Trixie the Knife Thrower

BEFORE A BIG DREAM COMES TRUE

Do you know what happens in the physical world right before a really big dream comes true?

Not a dang thing.

So if right now nothing seems to be happening in your life, take it as a sign. Which is meant to reassure you that if you sometimes wonder and worry if it's your "time"—or even wish it—it's not. Like a current underwater, change comes without a sound, and any lull you may now be experiencing is just the calm before a storm of coincidences, happy accidents, and serendipities that will bring about your next thrilling transformation. Always, something wonderful is brewing.

Nor should you wonder and worry that you might be handicapped by co-creations that involved the poor behavior of others. For whatever has transpired between you, your inevitable triumphs will be even sweeter and the humblest of apologies are in the offing. Which is what the dead want to tell you next.

CHAPTER 5

WE'RE SORRY FOR ANY PAIN WE CAUSED.

Not only do those who adventure into the jungles inevitably get hurt, but invariably *it's by someone else!*

And more often than not, a loved one; sometimes even the one they loved most.

When the time comes, of course, you will learn that *you* sometimes hurt others as much as they hurt you. And that the ones you hurt were often the ones you loved the most. So naturally, from the lofty views of the afterlife where deep, natural empathy puts you in the shoes of those you hurt, you're overcome by wanting to share the truths that will ease their burden, change their focus, and send them on a happier way. The dead are truly sorry for any pain they may have caused in your life.

The Big (Life) Review

When the switch is flipped and the lights of time and space go out, another is flipped somewhere else and the lights come on in what you now might term "the unseen." You'd expect no less if you're on board with life being eternal, organized, and of divine intelligence. It certainly wouldn't be eternal darkness, without form. In fact, words like *vibrant, intricate, thrilling,* and *spectacular* pale next to the beauty and order that are now invisible to you from "the seen." And with such order and beauty, and given that life within the jungles is an adventure school, would you or would you not also expect a life review? A report card, a status check?

Indeed. You're coming along so quickly.

And can you imagine who will assign your grades?

Yourself. You created this whole thing, at least your part of it, so who else? Not that you're supposed to sit in judgment of yourself, but you probably will. Instead, the aim is to learn. To see. To understand. To soar.

Naturally, post-return, with your enhanced perspective, you'll not only be able to revisit everything that happened between your birth and death, you'll see and understand your role in its creation: your methods and madness, truths and lies, rationale and justifications, hits and misses . . . *everything,* to a depth and degree you can't now comprehend.

Even seeing how one of your lifetimes left off, setting you up for the choices and adventures of the next. How your life two times ago influenced your most recent successes. How friends from millennia gone by agreed to show up again, whether to play, tease, or taunt, and how you agreed to engage with them. You'll see why you were so good at math or perhaps music, why you hated history or the arts, where you were when you fell in love for the first time, the influences behind your unexplainable urges and fears, the likely ancient connection between you and the parents you chose, and the people you loathed and adored and why.

You'll radiate pure ecstasy over your every triumph and conquest, beam proudly for your bravery and valor, savor and relish your tolerance, celebrate your dogged perseverance and sheer guts; your compassion, empathy, and tenderness. And all you feel will be amplified 1 million times as you see *your* good perpetuated by others, rippling outward, your smile and strength contagious, spreading like a wildfire through space and time—indeed, into eternity, reaching more lives than you ever might imagine could exist.

"WHOOPS, I DID IT AGAIN"

Yet you'll also watch in near disbelief at the times when you were bathed in love, supported by angels, and pushed on to greatness with dominion over all things, yet because of your own naïveté, ignorance, or misunderstanding, you knew none of these things. And then you'll watch as you took it upon yourself to right perceived wrongs, correct sensed imbalances, and claim for yourself what others were too daft to give you. Trying to effect change by manipulating the illusions and other people rather than going within. Being critical, judgmental, and hurtful—mentally, physically, and emotionally—while surrounded by a loving, adoring Universe. *Huh! Me?* You'll wonder, stupefied, whether the images have been distorted, because you remember all of the hurt and confusion you felt in those times but none of the love that surrounded you.

Such instances will be few and far between compared to your finer moments; nevertheless, they'll cause discomfort. In spite of so much support, in spite of how obvious it always could have been, you allowed yourself to go "caveman." And your remorse will be amplified as you see that your actions became excuses for others who cowered, blamed, and withdrew from the infinite possibilities of their own lives. And then you'll see how *their* actions cast shadows over an ever-expanding circle of others.

Ain't pretty.

Yet . . . you're strengthened by the "good." You see it expanding wider and faster than the "bad," bolstered by everyone's more powerful inclination to choose love. You see that there's time within eternity for all to majestically rebound. That nothing goes wasted and every experience expands God. That everyone eventually learns whatever they came to learn and returns to love; that everyone makes it "home," whole and complete, more than who they were. That there are an infinite number of second chances. And unmistakably, even as you see your greatest disappointments and mistakes, you feel that you're still absolutely adored. You *physically* feel it. And while you can't begin to understand this, you know it's true because *you're understood*. You know that everything is going to be okay. You understand that healing, for everyone, including you, is nonstop. *That the setbacks were foreseen as possibilities*. That everyone who crossed paths (or "swords") with you did so aware of the probabilities involved; they knew what might happen, and from the zenith of their brilliance they issued a commanding "YES!"

> Everyone eventually learns whatever they came to learn and returns to love.

HELP THEM HELP YOU HELP YOURSELF

But just as you wobbled, slipped, and made mistakes that brought pain to others, those who've done so to you are deeply sorry for the interactions in which you suffered. Interactions, in fact, that made it possible for them to see what they formerly couldn't. The dead are pressed all the more in gratitude to help those in pain halt or completely avoid a series of unfortunate events, especially as they now see what you can't: how easy it is, how strong you are, and how much more life has to offer those who let go of the past.

A Series of Unfortunate Events

If you, dear reader, are in a place of continued pain "caused by" others, living or dead, these tips can swiftly change your orbit to one that is more peaceful, loving, and fulfilled.

Groundhog Day (without Bill Murray)

Don't dwell on the past. It draws your attention away from all that's happening in the present. *Plus* it ensures that each of your subsequent life experiences will be tainted by the trauma of whatever was once said or done. Which will only trigger negative feelings, which will trigger negative behavior and choices, which in turn will trigger more negative manifestations. What goes around comes around (as in your thoughts coming around into more of those things you don't like). Just as the rich get richer and the poor get poorer, the bitter grow more bitter, with ever-expanding reasons to be bitter. Dwelling upon what once hurt you will only bring new surprises, new losses, more disappointments—*new reasons* to be hurt.

Leave Reruns to TV Networks

Your recovery is further impeded, and unpleasant manifestations compounded, when *your own focus on the past* invites the misguided sympathy or well-meant overattention of those who want to demonstrate their compassion by confirming that what happened to you was indeed awful, destructive, immoral, disgusting, shameful, harrowing, damaging, icky-gross . . . and that's just their warm-up. All of which, *if you play along,* only serves to create or confirm misbeliefs in your power-lessness, vulnerability, and victimhood. The "if you play along" part of that last sentence is all-important.

Now that you're discovering your power, you may wonder, *What about my negative friends/spouse/co-workers? Must I dump them?* Of course not. They obviously have some great qualities, too, or you never would've been their friends or married them, right? You like the same movies, laugh at the same jokes, and basically have fun together. You aren't as corruptible as you think. Just don't let their thoughts become your own. Don't abdicate this highest of all responsibilities: to think for yourself. You're learning this. Your inner powers are consolidating. By all means, defuse the negative chatter when you can, but whether or not you succeed, don't play along. Far more importantly, realize that no one else's moaning, lamenting, or complaining can change the new life track you're on. You are unstoppable now, naturally more positive than negative, inclined to suc-ceed, and born to thrive. *Olé!*

Fighting Phantoms

Seek not to fix or change others, especially when they've hurt you. Neither should you find excuses for their behavior or blindly "learn to love them"—however good a sound bite the latter makes. What will serve you most is to create as much space as possible within which to heal, be distracted, and fill your life with new friends, ideas, and adventures.

Einstein said that problems cannot be solved with the same mind-set that created them. The same can be said for manifestations and *their* mind-sets. Instead of tangling with what has already been created, turn your attention away and create anew.

"No" is never forever. You need not make sweeping declarations of what you will or won't do, or who you will or won't see. Not that it'll be easy. Not that you won't often recall better or worse times from the past. Just do your best; it'll always be enough. And leave the past to your biographers.

How Not to Be Special

Those who have *never* been seriously violated usually take it for granted that everyone has challenges—after all, *they* have challenges. Those who *have* been seriously violated can fall prey to the illusion that everyone else pretty much has a "normal" life, comparatively challenge-free, and doesn't have to deal with the sometimes intense doubts and fears that plague them. This often leads the violated to draw the false conclusion that the violation is at the root of their every quiver, sensed inadequacy, or embarrassing awkwardness, further complicating their anguish.

If the violated could peek at the worldviews of others, they would be utterly shocked to find that *everyone has issues* comparable to their own post-violation issues. Not that the violations weren't horrible or unusual. Not that these events haven't changed their lives. Not to diminish the gravity of the offenses. But there's no such thing as an unchallenged life. And whether or not a person's challenges are visible to others, or greater or lesser than others may have experienced, doesn't change the fact that they exist. What happens between two or more people is a *co*-creation; what happens afterward—your reactions to what happened and your subsequent choices—*is solely your own creation*. It's not as important that you understand why or how you got involved as it is that you seize any gifts you can from whatever happened between you and the other person and use them to deliberately craft your life going forward.

> **The key to your freedom has been with you all along.**

Let the Legend Begin

This is what the "dead" want to tell those they've hurt. They're sorry, but you needn't wallow or waste any more time over the past. They're sorry for the obvious reasons, and equally for what is not obvious: spoiling your thinking, sending you on wild goose chases, and contributing to your difficulty in knowing that it's "normal" to doubt yourself. Everyone does. Everyone at times feels lacking, undeserving, or inadequate. *Everyone has issues; they're essential to the great adventure of life.* Including the very challenges you may now have, "compliments" of a prior violation. They seed dreams to overcome them that launch you into the world as a powerful, deliberate Creator. You are not vulnerable; you are indomitable. And you will know this faster and more surely than those who are not blessed to have as challenging a history.

The key to your freedom has been with you all along. You're an ancient gladiator of love and joy who jumped at the opportunity to visit earth during these formative years to help spark some new thinking, see what you might make of things, share a few smiles, and help others live deliberately as they discover that they are as awesome as you.

The old belief systems that were once a comfort to you for the excuses they made possible have been outgrown. They need to be shed, just as a cocoon that once protected a chrysalis must fall away for the butterfly to emerge.

Warm and Fuzzy but Limiting Beliefs

1. Time is fleeting; I may have only one chance to get things right.

2. Opportunity only knocks once.

3. The early bird gets the worm.

4. I must be on guard against evil.

5. Luck (or its absence) is an uncontrollable component of every life.

6. We are not the only ones who control our future.

7. Life is a test and then we die.

8. There are bad people in the world.

9. Random and unpredictable things happen in every life.

10. I could have been more except for what happened to me.

Beliefs Beyond Forgiveness

1. Time and space set the stage for a lifetime of creating.

2. Opportunity never stops knocking.

3. There are enough worms for all the birds.

4. There is no evil other than what I choose to see.

5. I create my own fortunes and misfortunes; my thoughts become things.

6. The Universe conspires on my behalf, wanting for me what I want for myself.

7. Life is part of an unending adventure.

8. Everyone is doing their best and is of good intent.

9. Within every situation there is meaning, order, healing, and love.

10. I am more because of what happened to me.

DROP THE BLAME; PREPARE FOR LIFT-OFF

With understanding flooding your senses more and more, a new irony appears on your radar:

Forgiveness is only necessary when first there's blame.

The second lie needs the first lie. Withdraw the blame and forgiveness becomes a moot point.

To cast blame means to not understand that you create your reality, and such a blind spot can rob you of your power to live deliberately today and in the future. It prevents you from accepting responsibility for shaping the rest of your life. After all, if someone could randomly wreak havoc in your life before, which is what blame implies, it could happen again! When there's blame there's a belief that bad things can happen to good people for no reason. *You don't want to believe this any longer.*

Yet it's no wonder forgiveness is such a challenge in the world today: people believe the illusions are real and circumstances can randomly render you damaged goods. They can't. Nothing can. Not even yourself. The dead would have you skip the whole quandary from the gitgo and accept responsibility for everything. Then, with evolving clarity and more confidence in your power, you can also realize deep down that everyone is your friend, everything makes you more, and the sky is the limit for all you can still achieve.

REALITY CHECK

If this is indeed a chapter for you because of pain you've endured from earlier traumas and violations, and now you feel torn over which road to take, consider that none of what you've just read means the violator is off the hook. Violations are not okay. You did not deserve what happened. And each of your violators will one day have to "walk in your shoes." These points were made earlier, and because they're so important to understand, they'll be revisited later. To remain on point in this chapter, those who have hurt you, who've now moved on, are sorry. They want you to know this. They want you to live again.

They want you to know that it's okay to love life, love the process, love yourself, and to the best of your ability understand those who may still harm you, not because they deserve it *but because you do.* This is how to claim your rightful power. Your tormentors, past, present, and future, are lost in their own confusion and anguish. They didn't set out to hurt you, but to make some sense of a world that was hurting them. Your earlier thoughts—whether of confusion or love—combined with their thoughts, and the lessons for each of you began. You've been learning what serves you, and they've been learning what serves them. You each made this possible for the other.

> **Those who have hurt you are sorry. They want you to know this. They want you to live again.**

Understanding them doesn't mean you have to stay with them, heal them, or even give them the time of day. It may mean reporting them to the police, meeting them in court, or becoming their teacher, whether from a distance or through others. It means remembering that they, like you, are doing their best and that the two of you are just learning what works and what does not.

GREAT GETTING GREATER

Life is *not* just about learning tough lessons, but the last two chapters have been the hard ones. There are easier and happier ones to follow. You wanted it all, remember? Not just the candy-coated edition. Besides, even the hard chapters, when read through with eyes wide open and seen for what they offer, brim with excitement and possibilities, laying to rest old notions that truly robbed your thunder.

You didn't choose to be the person you now are *only* to be put through the mill. You came here to discover, play, and romance; to have best friends, hold hands, and whisper secrets into warm ears; to scale summits, ride waves, and gaze into a starry night. You wanted to rock *your* corner of the world. You did *not* come here for "some," "a smidge," or "a drop." You knew ahead of time that there would be circumstances that would make you cry, times you'd want to quit, people you'd like to throttle. Yet you also knew that these moments would be incredibly small prices to pay for the journey you'd have, the power you'd discover, and the love you'd share.

You also didn't choose to be surrounded *only* by adoring friends; you wanted guides, helpers, and teachers, too. You didn't want to learn slowly; you wanted the accelerated program. You're a love-being, and love-beings attract other love-beings. Yet given that these are the formative years on the planet, most do not yet know who they really are or how to handle all the power they have. To overcome this, you're helping each other, which sometimes means poking each other, biting each other, running with scissors, and the like.

There may be more lions, and tigers, and bears, although fewer and fewer as you become wiser and wiser. Some who go by the name of John, Pedro, or Lucas, or Sue, Aiza, or Olga—but not because there *have* to be. Not because suffering is the price of greatness or because good must bring bad, but because sometimes mis-creating is the price of learning how to co-create. Not because you're broken or you failed, but because you're great and getting greater. And not because you'll have *real* enemies, but because you'll have *real* friends: spiritual giants who love you so deeply that they'd go undercover for an entire lifetime as clods and ignoramuses to help you find out who you really are.

From a Dearly Departed

Dearest Lauren:

I don't know how to begin... "I'm sorry" is too much about me. It doesn't begin to consider what you endured.

"Thank you" seems grotesquely inappropriate. As if I received instead of took.

You loved me and you only hoped to be loved in return. Yet I used your love not only to gain access to your heart and life, but to exploit your doubts and fears. I used you against you.

Lauren, however pathetic this may sound, I had no idea of the depth of my ignorance or the chaos of its consequences until now. And worse, I see that even after I stopped taking from you, the harm I had done led you to blame and hate yourself and to wrongly believe that the world was cruel and unfair—keeping you from seeing the love, possibilities, and beauty that were always everywhere.

I thought everyone gets hurt by life, right? Everyone has to suffer. If I didn't hurt you, someone else would. If I didn't claim the upper hand, you would. And as long as I was doing the hurting, I thought that I wouldn't be hurt.

Every lying child is found out and so is every truth.

Ignorance is the plague of the times we lived in. It's the root of every evil act. Yet in this Garden of Eden where hope springs eternal, all are of God and nothing is wasted. Ignorance is like a flimsy spiderweb that temporarily holds us down and sometimes binds us together. In this web the violator and violated are drawn together with lessons to trade until, through compassion and understanding, they develop muscles that are strong enough to free themselves. Then love emerges and wings spread wide, lifting us into the light.

It's beautiful here, Lauren. Everywhere there's love. Peace. Acceptance. And above all, understanding. God is so great. I'm reluctant to tell you because surely it will seem unjust, but I'm learning to be happy. Truly happy. I get to try again. To live again. To love and be loved again. Everyone does. That's what it's all about. Mistakes are just steps on a pathway leading to more truth and therefore more happiness.

As real as is my grief over what I thought, how I behaved, and the effects on you, even greater is my love for you, more than you ever knew it to be. Greater than when we first met. Greater than its highest earthly highs. Greater because I am greater for having been humbled by the greatness in you. If not for you, I would still be lost.

Please, Lauren, you still have time. You're stronger than you know. See the love, possibilities, and beauty again. They surround you. You still have all you need within you to create all you want in the world. It's why you're still there.

I'm sorry. Thank you. I will love you forever.

Jackson

You Sought to Become Wise

Those who show up in your life do so through an invisible attraction and your tacit approval. They have the same focus, the same beliefs, and the same vibration, or ones that are complementary to yours. They need you to fulfill their "prophecies" as much as you need them for yours. They'll become your teachers, not because they're wise but because *you* seek to become so. Forgive others as you would forgive yourself. Or better, understand others and move into the freedom of creating the best of your life. It only needs your nod, as you will soon read in the next "thing" the dead want to tell you.

CHAPTER 6

YOUR DREAMS
REALLY CAN
COME TRUE.

As good as you now are at deducing truth, consider: if life was just about surviving, then how would you explain imagination? If it was just about sacrifice, then how would you explain desire? If it was just about thinking, reflection, and the ethereal, then how would you explain the physical world? Quite the case, eh?

Finally, if you *are* the eyes and ears of God, couldn't you, wouldn't you, dream up a place to rival Pandora in the movie *Avatar*? A place of adventure and intrigue, bursting with harmony and love, where you could communicate with the animals and be one with the planet as you learn to master the art of mind over matter? *You would! You so would!*

Welcome home! Planet Earth! Jolly good! Without question, it's the most exciting place in your corner of the Universe. With 100 million different species inhabiting air, land, and sea, each with its own mind-numbing traits and characteristics. And then there's you at the top of your self-defined "food chain" with dominion over all things, the freedom to think and therefore create as you choose, and dreams to remind you of what's possible, how far you can reach, and how much you can be, do, and have.

Don't you see that in this bastion of perfection, this oasis among the stars that *you* imagined, designed, and built, you *are by nature inclined to succeed?* With default settings of health, friends, abundance, and all things good? Haven't you noticed that what you go for, nine out of ten times, you get? And that the one time you don't, it's just part of your learning curve? Dearest

> **Go ahead, want it all. That's what it's there for.**

darling, those who have passed see better than ever that dreams really can come true—*and knowing this* might make all the difference.

Ignorance Was Bliss . . .

Even at the height of your planetary spiritual ignorance, which still pervades the world—worshipping idols, praying in question marks, talking to God as if "He" were deciding things, thinking that rocks can be depended upon but your imagination can't—*you've blown the lid clear off surviving!*

Two hundred short years ago, a modern home in New York meant one story, two rooms, planked walls of wood, a dependable roof, and a nearby outhouse. Today it might mean a virtual palace on the 100th floor of a skyscraper, encased by marble, glass, and bamboo, with amenities inconceivable just a decade ago.

One hundred short years ago, most of the world still thought that flying was for the birds, yet you now have a space station.

Ten years ago, people were using MySpace.

No wonder "dreams come true" is pop vernacular the world over—not only in the stories you tell but in the lives you lead and the people you idolize. You're in time and space to thrive, destined to do so, and it becomes inevitable *once you know, really know, that it's true!*

Wishful thinking? *Really?*

In your own life, have you not smiled way more than you've frowned? Laughed way more than you've cried? Had clarity way more than you've been confused? Had friends way more than you've been alone? Had health way more than you've been sick? Money, even, way more than you've been in the red? One of the recurring themes in this book is that you are *inclined to succeed,* and in this chapter you'll begin to see both how and why; that it's more than a way of looking at life, it's your reality.

Go ahead, want it all. That's what it's there for.

You Amaze

Even with the lights out and people still believing in fate, luck, and karma as deciding factors in their journeys through life, success, health, and joy are the rule, and fabulous progress is now underway. But why not see the obvious? Because until they're ready to see the truth, they won't see it. No matter what the evidence. Presently, global majorities choose to believe that "life is hard and people are mean," so this is what they see, even though this perception comes from focusing on exceptions rather than the norm. Yet so great is the inclination for consciousness to grow, prosper, and become more that they succeed in spite of themselves.

The "dead" want to tell you that you were born to soar, to achieve, and to grow. That this is not a sometimes thing, it's your very nature, as much a part of you as the urges to eat, drink, and multiply. It's a huge part of what you came here to do. To rock your life! Dreams spark adventures that spark challenges that make growth possible. Challenges, again, are not a sign of weakness but a confirmation that your dream is worthy of you. Your challenges are temporary, while their lessons are eternal.

ROLL ON, RISE ABOVE, LIFT OFF

Can you even imagine what's possible once you understand your inclination to succeed and the mechanics to make it so? Can you begin to see where things are headed? Aren't you ready? Aren't you motivated? Haven't you suffered enough, gone without enough, bled enough, sweated enough, cried enough? Can you also see how the bumbling of the past, in spite of its pain, has paved the way and made possible this awakening you're on the brink of?

Once blinders are raised and beliefs unchained, all will see what's been there since the beginning: that on your abundant planet there's enough of everything for everyone, opportunity springs eternal, and the reason the early bird and the late bird both get worms is that just showing up is the ticket! That life is easy, people are awesome, and whenever you don't like what you have, where you are, or who you've become, you can change it. That you're already in the winner's circle by your mere presence in these hallowed jungles. That whatever dues once existed were paid long ago. Here, now, today, you are pushed on to greatness in every moment. The system is rigged on your behalf—it's time to wake up and live.

Your thoughts are more than fuzzy little wispy-wisps. They perpetuate life as you know it; they are the shape-shifters of time and space, God particles that eagerly assemble with an intelligence of their own. Just as water evaporates under the proper conditions, just as fires ignite and continents slide, your thoughts strive to become the objects, events, and players of your life, filling the mold created by your imagination with people, places, and things. When you do your job, they do their job! You can have whatever you want.

Happily, everyone gets to think as they please; doubly happy, your "positive" thoughts are at least 10,000 times more likely to manifest than your "negative" ones. *Get this!* Your life is proof—we just went through this. How else can you explain the fact that you worry a lot, often focus on what's not right, and still have more dreams come true than nightmares? You are like a tidal wave of love and joy rolling through eternity, supernatural and boundless, who's arrived in time and space just briefly to check things out. Nothing can change who you really are, not a bad day, week, or year; no setback, heartbreak, or violation. You will roll on, rise above, and lift off—it's your very nature. There is no "maybe," "not sure," or "hope so." You are unstoppable, fun-loving, born to succeed, pure, eternal God energy. This is what the "dead" want you to know so you can do what you came to do: live your life to the absolute fullest.

Imagine that you've *already* received, done, or become that which you now desire. Do not imagine *how.*

THE MIRACULOUS MECHANICS OF MANIFESTATION

There are, *of course,* steps that virtually all physical manifestations can be seen to follow. Deliberately engaging their mechanics begins with knowing what they are. Becoming proficient enough to get consistent results requires practice. Critical to the process is knowing that you're never alone. You have an anxious Universe and supportive principles at your beck and call—not accidentally, but by design—nonjudgmental yet leaning in your favor because this is in alignment with the intention of the entire nonneutral Universe. You are it; you are adored; you are God becoming more, here to joyfully succeed.

Your job in bringing about change is the easy part. Just two steps are required for unleashing metaphysical energies and laws, bringing about what others will likely call miracles, luck, destiny, divine intervention, coincidence, and the like. And if you simply take both steps, and keep on taking them until there are results, as long as you aren't tripping over the nuances named in the following steps, thy kingdom or queen-dom must come. But you *have to* take these two steps even though it may *seem* that you're all alone, nothing's happening, and the odds are severely stacked against you.

Step 1: Define what you want in terms of the *end result*.

Mentally, in your mind, in thought, imagine that you've *already* received, done, or become that which you now desire. Do not imagine *how* this will happen. Do not worry about the logistics. Do not see the process; imagine it completed.

Step 2: Show up, every day, moving in the direction of your dream.

Physically, to any degree you can, do something. These are the baby steps. They *always* seem futile. You may be dreaming of champagne and caviar, yet you have to ride the bus to your interview at the mall. Do it anyway. It doesn't matter that you aren't sure if you're on the right path; chances are you're not. Do it anyway. If you have absolutely no idea of which direction to move in, move in *any* direction.

Your thoughts have an energy and a life force all their own. They move around the props, players, and circumstances of your life as if they were puppets on strings, predisposing you to life's so-called accidents, co-incidences, and serendipities. These will lead you into a world that ultimately, gradually, and seamlessly mirrors what you had been thinking about. Yet if you stay at home sitting on your couch with a vision board waiting for Oprah to call, there simply cannot be any accidents, coincidences, or serendipities. This is why you must physically act on your dreams, not to hit the home run or to do the hard part but to be within reach of life's magic. It rarely matters precisely what you do; because you've done something, a world with new possibilities is drawn to you.

Like GPS Navigation

Perhaps you can see this even better with the metaphor of GPS navigation. It's built into cars and smartphones and works in exactly the same way as dreams come true.

Step 1: Give the device your *destination* (end result).

Because it already knows where you are, as soon as you give it your destination the GPS knows *how* to get you there! In fact, in a split second it considers *every* road and highway you could choose from. It factors in speed limits, traffic lights, yields, merges, and often construction. And amazingly, in a split second, it then knows the shortest, quickest, happiest route! But notice, it doesn't start "talking" to you until you do Step 2.

Step 2: Put your car in gear (and roll).

If you don't put your car in gear, the entire system is wired *to not help you!* If your car remains in Park, you're actually telling it, "No. Not now. I'm not ready." Even if you don't know you're saying that, you won't be helped, because telling it where you want to go and then not letting it take you there is a giant contradiction. It's the same in life when you have dreams you don't constantly act on. In the car, once you're in Drive, the entire system flies into action, tracking your progress, rerouting you when necessary, virtually holding your hand until you arrive. Should you choose less than optimally, perhaps distracted by singing along at the top of your lungs to Barry Manilow, you'll eventually be put back on track with "Make a legal U-turn." You don't get such guidance and correction in either a parked car or a parked life.

THE MIRACLES OF PROGRESS ARE INVISIBLE

The miracles of progress are almost always invisible, but this doesn't mean they're not happening.

When you set out to change your life—or, to stick with our last metaphor, embark upon a GPS-guided journey, this time three hours long and to a new friend's home that you've never visited before—at what point in the journey does it become obvious that every left- and right-hand turn was spot-on, perfect, miraculous?

In the final seconds!!

Can you imagine the travesty, then, of concluding at 2 hours and 55 minutes into the journey, "It's not working for me . . . It works for everyone else but me . . . I must have invisible, limiting, self-sabotaging beliefs . . . I think I'll return home and watch *The Secret* 30 more days in a row"? No! It *does* work for you! It *always* works for you! Every day you get closer; every day it gets easier! Let these conclusions be your modus operandi forever more, on every journey. The moment you claim it's not working, *it stops working.* The moment you claim it's hard, it becomes hard. The Universe, your greater self, hears you. These become your new end results. It doesn't judge. It just responds. You cannot tell it one day, "I'm going to be a rock star" and the next day say, "It's not working" without these two opposing "end results" clashing and possibly canceling each other out. Yes, you're still inclined to succeed, yet why make it harder than necessary when sometimes a simple change in perspectives and words can so powerfully work in your favor?

THE NUANCES

Wheels don't generally roll up hills, fires don't usually burn wet logs, and dreams have a very difficult time coming true if they're dependent upon:

1. Specific paths (the cursed "hows")

2. Specific people (the cursed "whos")

3. Specific details

Specific Paths

Sometimes you'll succeed, but insisting that a specific path is *how* your dream will come true is messing with the "cursed 'hows.'" You put the weight of the world on your shoulders, creating stress, fostering worry, and worse, limiting an otherwise unlimited Universe. A Universe that is tracking each and every one of your 60,000 unique thoughts per day, as well as those of 7 billion other co-Creators. And not only are all of these thinkers prone to change their minds and rearrange their life priorities on the fly, but all have dozens if not hundreds of other dreams, desires, and wishes that are also added into the equation of every new second in time and what it will physically contain. The Universe, therefore, needs flexibility and freedom, just as anyone would who's negotiating an obstacle course filled with swiftly changing parameters. Yet as soon as you say, "I must make my fortune from this book I will write," you slam the door shut on all other possible ways for making fortunes. Not that you can't possibly have both, but as soon as you see X as the only way you can have Y, you're skating on thin ice, with *infinitely fewer* paths for success.

Specific People

Again, *sometimes you'll succeed,* but you simply cannot make specific people behave in specific ways unless they let you. Not your romantic partner, business partner, clients, customers, children, parents, employer, or employees. They have the built-in protection you also have—that your life, options, and power cannot be infringed upon—however to the contrary this may often seem.

This by no means prevents you from having an amazing romantic partner, business partner, clients, customers, and so on; it merely means you can't specifically insist upon who they must be. Turn it over to *divine intelligence,* who knows all such possible matches.

As a parent or an employer, you have a responsibility to guide the behavior of those specific people who need and want your guidance. But even as you work to maximize the chances that they'll behave as you would have chosen, there's still no guarantee they will. Know this, and do not hang the star of your happiness upon their choices.

Specific Details

Details are a dime a dozen, and no matter what they are, no matter how sexy, fun, and compelling, they're all unimportant. This doesn't mean your life won't always be filled with details or that those details that show up won't thrill and excite you. But when you insist upon or attach to any particular details, whether part of a bigger picture or not, there will likely be stress, limitation, and perhaps bitter disappointment. First, understand that specific details are relatively unimportant to the grand scheme of your being. Second, know that if those details are too entwined with specific paths and specific people, they may similarly jeopardize the entire manifestation.

As was true of the specific hows and specific people, if you insist on specific details *sometimes you'll succeed.* Especially if there's a lot of what you want available, like red roses or a particular year and color of a Volkswagen

Beetle—you'll probably get them. But for a particular house on a particular hill, or a gold medal at the next Olympics, understand that when there's only one of something and lots of people want it, many will be upset if they put off their happiness until they get it. There's absolutely no need to give importance to items that exist in scarcity *when what you really want is more happiness, more health, more love, and more abundance, of which there's enough for all.*

Attempting to micromanage your greater successes by first stacking up or collecting details is essentially the same as messing with the "cursed 'hows.'" Let 'em go. The brain's too small; it wasn't meant to do this. Yes, the details rock—definitely think of them, visualize them, love them—*just don't insist on or attach to them.* This is not hard to do. Leave room for even better than you could have imagined. Let your end results be happiness, health, prosperity, or other ambitions that have sweeping implications for the "time of your life" without attachment to trinkets that will, all on their own, inevitably show up at the right time, in the right way.

Here's how you can dance with the nuances, yet without attachment:

Imagine driving Bruno and yourself, in your new red BMW, with a dozen yellow roses in the backseat, on your way to LAX airport, to fly Upper Class on Virgin Atlantic to London Heathrow, on the first leg of an around-the-world trip, to celebrate the opening of your new hula-hoop factory in Mobile, Alabama. But as you go on living your life, metaphorical car in gear, showing up and taking action, don't lock out other possibilities. Remain open. Knock on lots of doors. Start writing your book, too, go back to school, circulate your résumé, try real estate sales, join an Internet dating site, and never stop being available to life's magic and miracles while obviously considering your strengths, likes, and preferences every step of the way.

It might not be Bruno, London, or the factory, after all. It may instead be Rocky, Rome, and your new yoga empire. The details should only get you excited about your end results, they should not *be* your end results. Attach to the big picture, your exciting new life, and surrender to all else while constantly showing up.

Resist the temptation to bite into the apple from the Garden of Eden, which was only ever a metaphor for behaving as if the illusions of time, space, and matter were more real than that which gave them rise. Don't eat of the forbidden fruit by seeing circumstances out of context, as if the paths, people, and details must be managed to get what you want. Instead go within to their source: your imagination.

You've Been Misled—by Your Physical Senses

By now you can probably appreciate that if someone believed "life is hard and people are mean," this would be one of their unintentional end results, Step 1. It's not that they *want* the world to be the way they believe it is, but desire or aversion alone is not the determining factor in any manifestation. What matters is that the thoughts are thought and then, Step 2, they are acted upon.

Acting upon end results doesn't just mean going out to try to make them happen. Sometimes your collateral behavior will tip the scales toward hastening a manifestation. If you believed life was hard and people were mean, collateral behavior might include stockpiling, locking doors, guarding your heart, and so on. And while such precautions would seem to ward off "evil," energetically, they'd actually invite it. "As a man thinketh, so he behaveth," increasingly ramping up the energy and a sense of expectation, and eventually those thoughts become things. With such a manifestation, you'd have cause to think and behave further along the same lines and a cycle would be born.

Every time you ventured into the world, things would shift around to show you "hard and mean." Even if you made some major life changes—got a new job, relocated, whatever it might be—if you kept the same old "hard and mean" worldview, "hard and mean" would follow you. Annoying circumstances and difficult people would be invisibly and serendipitously drawn to you, and you'd see this barrage of "bad luck" as proof that "life is hard and people are mean"!

Unless you were extremely observant and inquisitive, it would take many disappointments, coupled with a growing awareness that not everyone was having your same experience, before you'd even consider that it was yourself who was attracting such unpleasantness (after all, *you're a really nice person!*). Feeling brokenhearted and lost, however, will slowly lead the most stubborn souls inward to reflect and consider, *What's really going on here?* Leading to the gradual realization that they themselves—their thoughts, their imagination, their prayers (*thinking and talking about* what they want and don't want), their worries, their expectations and beliefs—might be the source of their experiences.

> **Your dreams are yours for a reason: to make them come true.**

And that therefore, if they want to create change they must begin with themselves, reconsidering what they think, believe, and expect—*even while, at first, the world is still showing them what they used to think, believe, and expect.*

LIFE'S ONLY VARIABLE

Any life is a series of journeys, each sparked by dreams that physically send you out into the world from which things and circumstances, and then emotions, arise. You have no control over the fact that you *are,* that you think, that you create, and that you will have journeys. But you can pick and choose your thoughts and thus your destinations, to shape the journeys they in turn create, and thereby extract more of what feels good and less of what doesn't.

What makes you *you* boils down to what you think, which leads to what you'll feel. Call your thoughts "decisions" or "words" or "actions" or "intentions": it's still the same. Thinking is all there is; it's life's only variable— not *that* you will think, but *what* you will think. You have the choice to intentionally craft the journey as it unfolds, or to unintentionally craft it. You can choose to steer the vessel that contains your heart or let it drift across the sea.

DANCE YOUR DANCE

Follow your heart. This is your purpose. You have desires; admit them. Listen to them. Choose to bring them to life. Your dreams are yours for a reason: to make them come true.

Dance to the beat of your own drummer. Every day, dance. The sooner you start, the sooner you'll find your rhythm in the symphony of 7 billion other dancers. And as you choose your dreams and learn their moves, remember that for every baby step you take, you increase, *exponentially,* the Universe's chances of reaching you quicker and in ways more to your liking. Every day, move, take action, go out, even when—especially when—you don't know what to do or how your dream will come true. You don't have to know how. You can't know how. Do anything. The Universe will find you, dots will be connected, and life on earth will be as it is in heaven.

From a Dearly Departed

Bobbi, Julie, Timmy!!!
I'm here!! It's Momma!!
Lordy, I've given up trying to talk—you just keep ignoring me. So I've decided to write.
You wouldn't believe where I've been. Time travel, space travel, you name it. Ever since I fell off the roof, the weirdest things have been happening. It's like one really long, far-out dream, except it makes sense ... and my wrinkles are gone! Some new friends keep telling me I'm dead, but I don't let that bother me. Usually they're real nice. Besides, they seem like the freaky ones to me. Like calling me "dead." Who does that? Right?

I've seen Grandma and Grandpa. They're young again! Ma's butt tattoo is finally gone and she's swimming every day. Dad's surfing the most humongous waves. We talked forever about the pyramids and how they were really built with sound, Atlantis and how it sank, and I learned all about the ant people . . .

I watched a movie of my life! Holy smokes! Talk about shocking! I relived being a child . . . saw you each being born . . . saw Daddy going to Vegas, instead of Denver . . . and . . . well, I knew it anyway . . . and I saw Richie do some really bad things in the name of really good things. But the one theme that kept repeating is how every accomplishment, every goal achieved, every dream realized, was somehow thought of or imagined in advance. And I mean everything—icky stuff, too. I didn't notice the connection before, but now it's so flippin' obvious!

Sometimes, of course, things happen that aren't imagined ahead of time, but it's always to fast-forward someone's life to a place that can match their thinking. They call those EMs, Escalator Moments, here. Some are pleasant and some are not, but all are based on other thoughts of theirs.

Sometimes, things people think about don't happen even though they were thought of all the time, but this is because other thoughts of theirs that did become things got in the way. TBT, thoughts become things—whoo-hoo!

Oh, and the best part . . . anyone can have pretty much anything. Anything! Funny how we were always told that success requires sacrifice, dues to pay, luck, timing, college degrees, and that "it's not what you know, it's who you know." Ha! The thing I find hardest to believe is how gullible we were. I mean, just look at the people who succeed, or who have what I once dreamed of having!! Hul-lo, what was I thinking??

The only thing people who succeed have in common is that they dreamed of their success. They imagined it. Thought it possible. Did something about their dreams, and I'm not talking about working hard in most cases. Amble, stumble, or sheepishly move in those directions, and bingo! And just look at all the folks with money these days! Not a rocket scientist among them! Turns out there's no connection between making a fortune and brains——zero! Just look at the people who have money! Nor is there any connection between happiness and having a certain faith, background, ethnicity, or pedigree. Happy people think happy thoughts! It takes so little. They focus on what they like instead of what bothers them, what works instead of what doesn't work, and then they attract and receive more things to be happy about! Just like people who focus on their income and not their expenses start creating more income, and those who do the opposite get the opposite. Duh! Just like people who focus on health and not illness, love and not hate, traveling instead of staying at home, all get these things——it always works. TBT!

Well, if you guys don't reply to this, I don't know what I'm going to do, but I have to admit I miss coffee and sunrises. This place has everything, but it's not like being with you. I miss how things were. Maybe I am dead, just not gone ... Maybe ... I can come back ... maybe if I think about it more ... maybe if I imagine it ... maybe ... !!!

Any-who, loving you until the cows come home ... XOXOXO,

Your Momma Forever

IT'S STILL YOUR TURN

This is it! What you've waited millennia for! You're here!! Whatever you want, however you want it (barring the tiny nuances we've reviewed), you can have! Don't ask for one thing; give thanks for many. Don't wish and hope; declare and create! If you only knew, as you will know, as you can know right now, the entire world spins in the palm of your hand. Sure, there's more to life than living deliberately—like great friends, compassion, and the color orange—but when you know the truth, deliberate living is your ticket to smoothing out bumpy roads, spreading the wealth, and living comfortably and creatively, both emotionally and materially. This is what the dead want you to know about your life now, which will make for an even more impressive homecoming at which all will share in your tales of being the comeback kid, rags to riches, or however else you may like to paint the next scene. And speaking of impressive homecomings, get a load of the next thing the dead want to tell you.

CHAPTER 7

"HEAVEN" IS
GOING TO BLOW
YOUR MIND!

That white light you hear of people seeing during near-death experiences? It's love. Seen by "tired" eyes.

You sense both that it emanates *from* intelligence and that in some uncanny way it *is* that intelligence. You get that it *knows* you far better than you know yourself; it understands you; it adores you. Like a doting parent, times infinity.

> **This white light is as close to God as any of us can get *before finally knowing we are God.***

This recognition, being so understood, is "heaven." You also grasp that it was *your* misunderstandings that created the disconnect in the life you just left, preventing you from feeling what was there all along. This white light is as close to God as any of us can get *before finally knowing we are God.* In it you will marvel, with revelation upon stunning revelation, in total ecstasy, and then you will wonder how you might have lived had you always known:

- ☀ How important you were,
- ☀ How powerful you were, and
- ☀ That there were no mistakes.

Except, of course, because you're reading this now, you're about to find out.

How Important You Are

You are simply amazing. You see things that no one else will ever see. You hear things that no else will ever hear. You've gone and will go where no one else will ever go. And above all, you think and thus feel things that no one else will ever feel. This is who you are. This is *why* you are. These are your sacred offerings to the Highest of Highs, yet you need do nothing other than be. And by being, you create what none has, can, or ever will create. You are the face of God as it's never before been seen.

Adored? Words completely fail. Cherished? More in every moment, in an upward spiral without end. And this is what you begin to feel in the moment you arrive.

While "alive," most people measure who they are by what they're not. Don't wait until you die to see the whole truth. Nobody can be everybody. No one will ever have everything. Of all that God is, you are but a very small sparkle, which means if you go looking for what you are not, you will always find it. The point was never to find out what you are not but to find out what you are: a collection of traits, characteristics, leanings, desires, quirks, dimples, freckles, and ever more as you expand eternally, creating a priceless window on creation through which God, not through you but *as you*, both observes and commands the elements—and dances with Herself, as She appears as others.

You are one of a kind. You are *irreplaceable*. A masterpiece, a Mini-Me of the Divine sufficient unto yourself. *You* are a dream come true, God's first and last chance to be you, exactly as you now are. *Bask*; it's more than enough. Yet even as you might bask, you will be followed, honored, and celebrated by angels and admirers in the unseen, because even now, as you read these words, you are more important than you can possibly imagine.

How Powerful You Are

In the moment you arrive, you'll begin to see, as those who've come before you have seen, that life as you once knew it was the dream and that this "new place" is where you dreamt it from. And that as the dreamer, you were always bigger than the dream; and that even as you thought life was happening to you, you were happening to life. You came first. You were the reason, literally, that the sun rose each day.

Death will be the gateway to being more "alive" than you now suspect is possible. The sliver of reality that pertains to you suddenly increases exponentially, including past, present, and future. You'll find there are parallel earths each with a different version of yourself, each in existence because of a fork in the road of your former life in which you gave serious thought to both paths—at which point a literal wrinkle in time was created, a parallel universe was born, and you simultaneously went down both roads, each "you" thinking you were the only one.

You'll see that this "fractioning" occurred throughout your entire life, at *every* crossroads, small and large, where decisions had to be made. The smaller tangents usually merged back in, yet the larger crossroads often led to wildly different experiences, completely different lives, different careers, partners, children, lessons, discoveries, everything.

And in every version of reality there's you, at its very center, your thoughts, beliefs, and expectations. Living lifetimes within lifetimes by the hundreds or thousands, yet clearly each incarnation is . . . you . . . and this is all well before we've even considered how this affects your typical interpretation of reincarnation, "after" a lifetime.

Staggeringly, *all of this is powered by you! And you get it! It makes sense!*

Your present measures of power in terms of the illusions—volts, torque, lift, horses, thrust—bear no resemblance to how power is measured spiritually. Each man, woman and child alive in your world today is literally capable of moving mountains with just words . . . hence the expression. And one day you will.

Thy Kingdom Come

Your reach is more than you could have fathomed in time and space. Your history is far richer. Your people more amazing. And your spiritual power, which even now lies mostly dormant within you, is more than your brain can comprehend—which limits it not. You will reel in awe upon seeing what you've done and sensing what lies ahead, all because of your time *in* space. Gazing upon the physical landscapes of your recent life, you'll see how the illusions—matter and circumstances—bent to your every flight of fancy, daydream, and fear. That you arranged and then rearranged and changed again and again the props, players, and circumstances of your life almost as swiftly as you changed your mind. So almighty were you—and are you—that:

- ☀ As you stir in thought, winds begin to howl,

- ☀ As you smile, waves of love lap upon eternal beaches,

❋ As you speak, the floodgates of abundance and good fortune begin to tremble, and

❋ As you dream, the stars realign.

This is your life. Your power. Know it to use it. Begin today.

Because by design, as you inevitably prevail against odds, soaring in every area of your life, and success becomes commonplace, you'll start to wonder what else there is to know, how else there is to live, and what else you might be capable of. And because of your wondering, also by design, you'll become even more powerful and curious, and a magnet for even more knowledge, wisdom, truth, and love.

That you've already cleared a psychological pathway in these primitive times on your new little planet and in your formative years for "dead" people to reach you with such messages *mid-dream* is proof. Bloody well done.

THERE ARE NO MISTAKES

The sublime perfection of time and space is that everything that happens, *and everything that does not,* makes you more. So magnificent is this inherent formula that nothing can tarnish the beauty of the jungles of time and space. It's only your belief in the illusions, the little white lies that make your adventures possible, that tells you otherwise. Think about it. You have *forever.* You will live again and again. So wouldn't every seeming setback, loss,

Life as you once knew it was the dream, and this "new place" is where you dreamt it from.

or disappointment ultimately make even more mean-ingful future advances, gains, or triumphs? Mightn't they also serve as lessons to others who may then avoid any discomfort you experienced, so that your pain or sorrow may spare them the same?

And again, the illusions are just illusions; *they're not real*. It's only your belief in them being real—objective, black and white, all or nothing—that makes you suffer. From your new vantage point, looking back at your re-cent life will be like waking up from a vivid dream. *"Wow, that was incredible!!"* Particularly comforting when there were bumps. Yet the experience made possi-ble by thinking it was real changed you. Made you wiser. You have a new lease on "reality," so to speak, because the lessons of the dream were so impactful! So helpful! So attention-getting, jarring, beautiful, and spectacular! And such is life within the jungles of time and space from the perspective of an afterlife glance; nothing is real except the learning and love you take from them.

Perhaps you now wonder, "And what of those who are hurt, or worse, in their lifetime? Wasn't their loss so great that it irrevocably shattered any hopes that the rest of their lives could have been as happy as they would otherwise have been?" But then also ask, as we have been asking:

- ☀ Am I so sure there were no gifts that will ever come from what happened to them?

- ☀ Am I so sure that this is their only life?

- ☀ Are they not forever beings?

- ☀ Am I so sure I know where their life was headed prior to the "undesirable" occurrences, and that it would have been more favorable?

☀ Am I so sure what happened doesn't make perfect sense to them?

☀ Am I so sure their lessons on earth weren't otherwise done and "graduation" inevitable?

It's ironic, though understandable, that from your perspective now, within the illusions at this primitive time, the consensus is that the absolute worst thing that could ever happen to anyone is to die. Why? Because to your *physical senses,* death means to extinguish a life and all of its possibilities forever and ever. Curtain call. All done, except for, maybe, the supposed best-case scenario: some harp music until who knows when. Yet with a spiritual awareness, finally grasping that eternity precedes and follows every lifetime, it suddenly becomes obvious that those within the illusion should not be deciding, certainly not for others, when the optimal time to die might be. Perhaps the person with a deadly disease has chosen a slow exit after a very fulfilling lifetime, having learned all that he came to learn, so that he can say his good-byes, administer his last will and finances, and allow everyone to have some notice, rather than choosing a sudden stroke or car accident. It would be a bit awkward, then, if Aunt Sally and Uncle Billy were to round up the entire family and distant cousins to hold prayer vigils around the clock, asking that their beloved's disease be removed and his life extended.

The workaround is always to wish for the best for all involved without stating what that best might be, since you can never know what it is for other people. And then, whatever happens, know that it *was* for the very best because there are no mistakes.

The Order, Perfection, and Enormity

The kingdom, the glory, and the power . . . after your transition you'll be overwhelmed by all that is then knowable. And to offer more assurances of the beauty and miracles, here are some more of the "things that will make you go 'Hmmm'!"

The Truly Incomprehensible

Not even the oldest souls, the greatest angels, or the wisest guardians—at least not those within reach of time and space—can fathom the enormity of all creation or how it began: the leap from nothing to "All That Is." The original spark. How "God" came to be. How there could ever not have been "God." And just as mind-numbing, maybe much more so, how there ever *could be* "God." The essence of life itself, juxtaposed to "nonlife." Of course, wondering about the beginning presumes that time is a reality, because you can only have a "beginning" alongside the falsehoods of a middle and an end, creating the paradoxical question of starting points. Which brings up yet another seemingly impossible mystery: how does awareness/intelligence function in the absence of time? Time so handily gives you reference points sufficient to live an organized life. In fact, even to think as you now think, or to read as you are now reading, requires time.

Yet, keeping with our premise, much *can still be* observed, deduced, and known, and such insights begin revealing themselves at greater and greater speeds upon your transition, like bursts of twinkling lights at night in a festive holiday season.

The Divine Conundrum

While *how* the whole thing of time and space began *will* elude you, you'll suddenly and starkly see the *most* bodacious challenge accepted by every time-space traveler and already touched upon throughout this volume:

> To discern what's real in a sea of illusions; to trust their feelings in spite of contradictory physical evidence; and to see through the lies that have given them life.

Talk about a *dare!* Talk about an *adventure!* Upon your arrival, you begin to get that if "God" was challenged to devise the most outrageous interactive story, cinematic masterpiece, or Broadway show to include unrestrained drama, suspense, comedy, infinite possibilities, romance, and more involving every possible human emotion, condition, and expression, *it would be time and space!* Can you think of anything wilder than life in the jungles? Wider in scope? More compelling? More heartbreaking yet romantic? More dangerous yet safe? Complex yet so simple a child could explain it? Can you think of anything else so filled with hope that if you can dream something, anything, *you can be it?* So filled with tolerance that it doesn't matter where you've been? So filled with love that every path leads "home"?

Adventures into the jungles stir passion and create emotion: the main reason you've made the choices you've made throughout your life, including just to be present there. Yet, *optionally,* when one is ready to awaken mid-dream, *as you are,* it requires reflecting on your original, failed premise for how life works: that *things* (not thoughts) become things. Then you begin to understand:

- ☀ That what you dwell upon in thought, you'll meet in the flesh,

- ☀ That what you believe in, expect, and move toward *will begin moving toward you,* and

- ☀ That if ever you don't like what keeps showing up in your space, you can change it, by *changing yourself.*

Yeah, wow! But then, during this tsunami-size reveal brought on by your transition, you begin to imagine what it might have been like in your former life to consciously know you were a Creator . . . to know you were always where you most wanted to be, safe and sound as if in the palm of God's hand . . . to know you were powerful enough to make any dream come true, to choose love over fear in spite of appearances, and to be surrounded by ever-growing circles of friends and laughter. And as you ponder this, suddenly you're possessed with one huge, blazing desire: *to return, to go back, to dance among the illusions once again.*

Reincarnation (Sort Of)

Why not? After all, time is one thing you have lots of. Why, if given eternity, would anyone of divine origins choose to live just one lifetime? You have a hard enough time drinking one cup of coffee, enjoying one kiss, or eating one potato chip. We're talking *eternity.*

That means, if you lived 7-to-the-10-bazillionth-power lifetimes, once you were done, the amount of time you'd spent in body would be infinitesimal, invisible, *irrelevant* compared to eternity. Eternity is long, so why would you live just once? How about you live as many times as you want so you can be absolutely sure you've squeezed every last drop out of such an experience? You'd try out primitive times and high-tech times; you'd be born into poverty and into splendor. You'd be male and female; left brained and right brained; tall and short; aggressive and passive; brilliant and naïve; emotional and stoic; and countless other polarities *and combinations thereof!*

Then there'll be all the choices of where you might live: which planet, which country, which culture. And in each life you'll get to choose your parents, just as they will choose you, which friends from other lifetimes to play with again, and so on and so on. And everyone else is going to be in the same boat, wanting to come back again and again and again! Perfect! You'll return with those you learned well with and you'll avoid others. They'll be doing the same. Come on, you have forever. Why not?

Whoa . . . perfect . . . your celestial mind is churning!

Now to repeat, words slip and fail when it comes to painting pictures of reality. For instance, the simple idea of reincarnation immediately implies, *given your typical, bogus, one-time line worldview,* that after John Doe passes, he might come back as Jane Deer. The failed implication of this is revealed as soon as you wonder: Is the new Jane actually the old John, or is she Jane? Right, Jane is Jane! So where is John? John is still John! But didn't he come back? Yes, as Jane!

Consider, perhaps, that maybe one's personality is like a leaf on a soul-tree from which other leafy incarnations grow. And consider, perhaps, that since time is an illusion, all leaves play out simultaneously even though they also belong to different time eras. Now there's a bit more clarity *and* more slippage. Now we can see that John and Jane are not actually the same person, even though one has evolved from the experiences and wishes of the other and possesses some memory and *carryover of the other's lessons, experience, maturity, talents, and charms.* So there *is* something like reincarnation going on, but it's not just a linear progression of consciousness, with one incarnation ending so another can begin. Instead, each incarnation maintains its own perspectives eternally while simultaneously adding to the others. And while your mind is racing, let me add that it's quite possible—in fact it happens all the "time"—that someone's next incarnation will take place at an earlier point in "history."

> Even now you live your lives within God, yet you remain you.

The Fam'

Something of relevance and likely interest is that those presently "alive" in any planetary civilization inevitably belong to the same spiritual family, with far more in common than anyone ever suspects during the planet's primitive times. Even the stranger on a street corner is your spiritual relative, closest of kin. Even the stranger on a street corner halfway around the planet is your spiritual relative, as you two share the same approximate time and space from an infinite number of

possibilities. And as your life unfolds, you find there are some "family members" you particularly like to hang with (as was true with friends you like to learn with) and others you'd prefer not to see (or maybe even cause bodily harm to). Which is pretty normal in any family, right? And together, as a civilization, as one unit, one family, and just as One, you've ventured into the illusions and co-created your earth to be the playground and laboratory of your spiritual evolution—during which you'll live out some cool stories, reexperience your majesty, fall in love again and again and again, and have some fun.

Where Is Everyone Coming From?

As you begin assimilating the information extravaganza you're receiving in "the unseen," you'll immediately wonder cute questions such as "Where are all the people coming from?" For instance, if the earth had a hypothetical population of 1 million people 12,000 years ago, and now there are 7 *billion* and counting, "Where did they come from? Wouldn't there always be the same number?" Or you may wonder things like "If I am just an emissary of my soul, will I cease to exist upon my 'return'?"

But you'll quickly find that in this new, heightened afterlife perspective you can often spontaneously answer yourself:

- ☀ "As if," your first question innocently presumes, "there were no other life-sustaining planets."

- ☀ "As if there were no parallel and tangent realities."

☀ "As if there were no other realms I could 'occupy,' like the one I'll actually be in upon my dazzling arrival."

☀ "As if I hadn't just read and understood a moment ago that the desire to 'return' as Jane Deer does not diminish John Doe."

☀ "As if time and space weren't some sort of holographic, multidimensional dream."

☀ And finally, the coup de grâce: "As if there were only one time line to put everyone on!"

Similarly, you'll see that the idea of being swallowed into oblivion by your soul could only happen in the finite (and not real) world of time and space, with its dichotomies of here or there, now or never, and the like. This fear implies you cannot be in two places at the same time; that you must either be the "you" that you know or be absorbed by your soul. But blending does not have to also mean dissolving, as if you were to suffer the same fate as a sugar cube dropped into hot tea. In the case of "soul reunification," the personality remains intact while simultaneously adding to the entire whole. Both existing, eternally, *internally*. After all, there's no such thing as external in terms of reality. Even now you live your lives within God, yet you remain you.

Soul Ages

As you might imagine, as an individual or, perhaps better, at a soul level, this cycling in and out of time and space may get rather tedious after 10 to 50 *thousand* lifetimes. Goals are achieved, patience acquired, empathy cultivated and whatnot, and a complacent attitude develops. You will have fallen in love and been of service a million times, deeply, passionately, and genuinely, so you'll eventually think about moving on. This only makes sense, right? Not that you must "leave"; besides, you can only "leave" if you believe in "space."

You will ultimately try on for size every hat imaginable, progressing in maturity as you go. Starting out as a baby soul, comparable to a baby human in terms of awareness—helpless, confused, and often having no concept of right and wrong. Maturing into a young soul, comparable to a human child—bright, clumsy, and eager for life. Then on to becoming a mature soul, like that of a young adult, with dreams and newfound challenges—a highly productive and wisdom-fertile time of life. Finally moving into the phase of old soul, like that of a wise and seasoned veteran of life—reflective, tranquil, and highly considerate. Each incarnation bringing with it the lessons, experience, maturity, talents, and charms acquired earlier, just as a young adult will maintain skills learned in his youth, until, with mastery, you no longer have the same interest in the jungles compared to the new opportunities that lie beyond.

There is no better or worse soul age, as there is no better or worse human age. Each offers possibilities that the others do not, and all are necessary for the others to exist and have meaning. And while over your recorded history you will usually be able to see the slow evolution of the masses into "higher" and more refined living, making wiser choices centered in love, your time line does not have to contain your evolution. Meaning that one new soul's first incarnation could conceivably be in the year 125,589 B.C. and another's might be in A.D. 2014.

Collective Ages

Just as an individual matures, so does the collective. And in case you were wondering what the 2012 hubbub was all about, it marked a turning point in our mass spiritual evolution, passing through the tail end of the exciting "teenage" years of soul wisdom into the "young adult" years. A weighted average, if you will, of our fam's progress through the ranks. Naturally, some individuals grow faster, others slower; some gain more in a single lifetime than others will in 500. Consider also that we've not all lived the same number of lives. Yet all in all, we're still a bunch of big kids.

We're moving from the "Rah, rah, I rock! Hey, everyone, watch me!!" phase to the morning-after, hungover, ego-bruised phase. And for the first time understanding that we and we alone are accountable for the consequences of our every decision. Thus now, as we emerge from the formative years in which we learned to exercise our power, we're learning to be responsible with it. The inner mental resistance to such a transformation is what created—and still could create—the physical turmoil that's manifested in the form of earth changes and sociopolitical upheavals. Because, of course, the weather gets its drive, as all things seemingly inanimate do, from us. People don't much like change, especially if it challenges their worldviews and calls for them to be more responsible. The greater the inner storms of resistance, the greater the outer storms upon the planet, not as retribution, but as a plain and simple manifestation of the tension that's brewing within.

With a planet of newly matured souls (not *that* mature), and of course some new and old ones, too, there's still lots of drama, imparting lots of lessons. All in all we're moving along at a healthy clip, given the countless advances and relative calm on the planet. Sure, there's massive room for improvement, and there will be improvement. That's what this is all about. Although it's fascinating to speculate about where it will all lead, which not even the dead know, what's most important is honoring the forgotten choices that have brought you to each day by living with an open mind and an open heart, following your dreams. Wonder about the bigger picture, daydream and consider, but not to the degree of allowing what you don't know to distract you from what you do and can know.

THE RAPTURE

Each time you return "home" after an incarnation for the new lessons learned, fun had, and wisdom gained, you're able to recall more of the truth and see wider folds of reality. Like surfacing from an underwater dive, suddenly, as your head breaches the surface, there's air, the sun above, and a drastically increased ability to function; you've returned to your element. The same thing happens upon death. The exceptions would be extreme cases of terrified young souls who are so overwhelmed with their last life or its final moments that they require immediate guidance.

Suicides may also meet with different experiences, given the naïveté of their decision to end a lifetime—one, like all lifetimes, they had so meticulously planned and dared to choose, that would've ended "soon enough," naturally, had they let it run its course. Given their shortsighted-and-narrowmindedness, they usually lack the faculty to fully appreciate their new environs. Plus, rather than advancing to higher plateaus, they soon find they have to (and will eventually most want to) create new circumstances, vis-à-vis a new lifetime, that will better teach them what they had earlier refused to learn.

Otherwise, new arrivals, after life review and deep reflection, soon move into a state of euphoria and clarity far beyond what's shared in the near-death accounts of those who have not fully gone through the homecoming process. The perfection sensed is indescribable. You're in a place:

- ☀ Where everything that was ever broken is made whole;
- ☀ Where everything that was ever lost is found;
- ☀ Where everything that ever hurt has healed;
- ☀ Where there was once illness, there is health; confusion, there is clarity; despair, there is excitement; lack, there is abundance;
- ☀ Where everything that was ever feared is unmasked;
- ☀ Where every enemy is befriended; and essentially

☀ Where everything that was ever unpleasant
in your last life can now be seen with
understanding to be a great and fabulous
gift.

Loved ones who've passed welcome you. The most
joyful tears begin to flow. Friends and beloved family
members from *other* lifetimes "arrive" and are greeted
with instant recognition and a total remembrance of
times together. You're in a place to plan second chances and new romances, where there's a sublime glowing
grace that emanates from everything and everyone.
Where you truly discover what infinite possibilities
mean, where you can do less to get more, and the only
sweat involved in making dreams comes true comes
from dancing all night at the afterparty. Yes, this is real.
It's all real. You remain physical yet ethereal, your identity secure, just made more. Time and space still exist,
yet they're not the same in this world where everything
is pliable, forgiving, permissive. Your mind is blown to
pieces with joyful "aha's!" "oh boy's!" and "you gotta be
kidding me's!"

This is like home, or at least a gigantic step in that
direction. This is where your pre-earth life choices were
made, and here you'll see all that was gained. This was
the kingdom you distantly recalled while on earth, for
which all time-space is fashioned, in which you and all
others constantly strove to re-create—to keep you busy
and in action and living through the emotions that
would come from the ride. You'll find that your thoughts
in this world similarly become things, yet more artfully
and sometimes spontaneously; like everything else here,
your new manifestations will seem to sparkle in love

and shine with intelligence. You are now where the concepts of friendship, travel, communication, exploration, curiosity, adventure, sexuality, and *all that you had on earth* were first born and where they exist in the ethereal, at a level almost unrecognizable to your newly overloaded senses. This homecoming reacquaints you with *you,* your true self: an intergalactic love-being of joy and divine origins. You understand that it was from this perspective, this known zenith of your existence, certainly among others still unknown, that you chose to venture into the jungles of time and space, *and you knew what you were doing!*

You'll shrug, you'll wonder, and you'll gasp, first in disbelief and then over the inevitability of it all. Like water to parched lips or a glimmering of light to those lost in the dark, your senses will be flooded with relief and then rapture, followed by a longing to share the goodness and the beauty and the love with those left behind. And while you're comforted knowing that all of this awaits them, you feel impatient. And as you reflect in this love and consider that what you are now feeling was within reach during life—yes, this is when it hits you: more than anything else, you want to go back. To "live" again, to remember *this time,* to see what's so obvious, to find what you missed before, to reject the limiting confines that others want to "protect" you in, to honor yourself, to be true to your dreams, to risk your heart in love again, to be with those who so loved you, to walk barefoot on cold morning grass again, to sit before a campfire and gaze at faraway stars. To be a light

> Dreams come with built-in challenges; challenges come with built-in dreams.

to others, to rebound, come back, stand tall, and never stop loving it all *from within the mind of man!* Until the entire cycle of incarnations is complete, everyone wants to return—and everyone does.

Life is so beautiful, *your life* was so beautiful. Everything is a gift, you've always been adored, and you'll see this more clearly than ever through the looking glass you now call death.

From a Dearly Departed

Alejandro!!!

Everyone's here!!! *Everyone!* And they're all happy, healthy, and gorgeous!

Your mom says she's sorry. Your dad says he's proud of you. Even Gina's here, and she said to tell you she's still jealous you left her for a man . . . me! Thanks again, by the way. Don't worry—she's over it. Who wouldn't be when you come to a place like this and everything starts to make perfect sense! Choices galore, friends and family, colors and textures, sounds and aromas. Did you know that the reason there are only three primary colors on earth is that time and space there are so flat? Here, just within your first 21 days, give or take an eon, you learn of at least 42 dimensions—and there are more! There are hundreds of primary colors and all of them can be heard! Did you know that all colors have numbers? And that all numbers have sounds? And that all sounds have flavors? Mix the right colors together here and you have a musical ice-cream rainbow! Oh, and the number line here? It goes sideways, in ways, out ways, around ways! And there are actually "branches" off of every number, no matter which way, and . . . Actually, I had to stop that "download"; it was messing up my rediscovered angelic countenance.

You're going to just die . . . again, when you get here!

The only thing missing . . . is challenge. Oh, it's here for those who are moving beyond, but for the rest of us, chillin' between lives, we miss it. Not that much, yet. It's awesome to have none of the stress that we put ourselves through in the illusions. Like a vacation on steroids, but no steroids. Everything is so effortlessly spectacular. Some stay for thousands of years at a time. There's no schedule. But all either go back or move on—all. And here's a weird-y: there's no moving on until you're okay with going back.

Moving through the jungles means coming to peace with them. Which means coming to peace with yourself. Learning to deal with challenges is how you learn this, finding you're bigger than whatever you create or find yourself in. Which you can't learn, of course, unless you go back because there are no challenges here. See what I mean? Ironically, however, being bored with one's life is not a sign of peace but of not sufficiently challenging oneself. Usually it's the happy person, busy person, socially comfortable person who's nearing the option to move on.

Did you know that if it weren't for challenges, life as we knew it wouldn't be worth living? If in every life you chose to be born to wise, loving parents in technologically pampered times, always with a high intellectual and emotional intelligence quotient, good looking, coordinated, and popular. E-w-w-w! Fun for a few times maybe, particularly if previously you'd had a challenging lifetime, but after a while, you'd want more, you'd want it all—not just the bling but the passion. Usually, you'll see, having more comes from starting with less.

Which doesn't mean you have to be scared or really uncomfortable in a life to have great gains. It just means you have to be growing. Which is where dreams take you and why you have them. Dreams come with built-in challenges; challenges come with built-in dreams. The parameters that begin each new life are chosen for exactly these reasons. In other words, lives are chosen for the challenges they will likely present, or to flip this, for the dreams you will likely have. Same-same. Kind of explains your dad, huh?

Alejandro, I love you so much. My feelings are indescribable and almost unbearable, except that being here I'm supported by the light that's everywhere, so even as my heart is full of longing for you, I couldn't be any happier. I know we'll be together again, forever, that we are connected, and that you and I and everyone else will know this ecstasy of being that has now overcome me.

It's beautiful here, so beautiful, but it is there, too, and I'm going to see you soon. Yet until we share the same vibration again, mon chéri, be happy. Whatever it takes, whatever you need, whoever you want—be happy. Which means follow your dreams, face your fears, and every single day move forward. Happiness is my only wish for you, and I am at peace knowing you will have it.

Your handsome savage,

Freddy

WAIT ONE MINUTE, BUCKO!

It's all so glorious! So much peace, harmony, and beauty! So much love! You never had *anything* to fear—not for yourself and not for those you miss. Which is what this "thing" is that the dead want you to know about *living!* But fresh from the jungles, no matter how sublime the afterlife is, you will surely want to ask your welcoming committee about the greatest seeming contradiction of all: "Why *on earth*, literally, do bad things happen to good people?" To which they will reply in the coming chapter.

CHAPTER 8

LIFE
IS MORE
THAN FAIR.

Understanding is the elixir of life, the soothing balm that helps dry tears and erase wrinkles. No one's judged for their shortsightedness, but they *are* severely handicapped by it, whereas the enlightened one, far from being your stereotypical hermit, can run faster, jump higher, and has more friends, laughter, and abundance. Hence the joyful urgency the "dead" have for reaching you with insights that reassure and inspire.

The sage doesn't feel sorrow in parting, whether it precedes days or lifetimes of absence. He knows that to think of someone is to be with him, while the space created will make possible new adventures. He knows that any separation the eyes perceive is a lie. The prophet does not feel anger at betrayal. She saw it coming. She understands that for some, the need for recognition can be greater than their desire to serve. And she knows that her own happiness and greatest mission do not depend on the behavior of others. The mystic does not blame or find fault in others because, seeing himself as a Creator in a world of illusions where nothing happens by chance, he knows that all pain is self-inflicted and that life is fair, even when circumstances are not.

> "Hey, sorry, the earth is so huge, you can't have fair *all of the time,"* said Divine Intelligence, never.

WHY DO BAD THINGS HAPPEN TO GOOD PEOPLE?

Wouldn't it seem, considering the splendor of it all—10 sextillion suns, 100 million exotic species, the splendor of a mere lone *apple*—that the "mind" behind it could have somehow created stopgap measures or instituted mechanisms to prevent unexpected, pointless, bad things from happening? At least from happening to *good people?* Like a dog's "no barking" collar (hideous things), what if before people think, speak, or behave hurtfully toward others they receive an electric shock? Wouldn't that work?

Or is ugly the price of beauty? Is violence the price of peace? Is hate the price of love? Does that make sense?

Does it?!

Or maybe, as religions have taught, evil exists unto itself as some primordial earthbound nebula or ugly energy mixture, with a will and intelligence of its own, lurking in paradise like a cockroach in God's kitchen? Fueled and sustained by . . . well, no one ever thought to ask. Insufficiently capable of taking over all good things, however depraved, yet invincible enough to stand its ground and hold its own before *"God."*

Does that make sense?!

Are either of these ideas remotely plausible when you consider . . .

- ☀ That there are birds who *sing* for ears that can hear at every hour of the day and night?

- ☀ That there are creatures of the deep that flip, twirl, and leap just because it's fun?

- ☀ That there are "furry friends" who love just as *dearly* as they are loved?

- ☀ That there are flowers so exquisite, pleasing human eyes could be their only explanation?

Actually, *mustn't* these splendors surely prove that you're now living in the most magical fairy tale ever imagined, with no need or place for an errant bogeyman?

"Hey, sorry, the earth is so huge, you can't have fair *all of the time*," said Divine Intelligence, never.

Check Your Premises

Could there have been some kind of celestial oversight? Some mistake? Have things spun so out of control that the earth now exists in a range of probabilities that the Divine never foresaw when the first star shone brightly in the night sky?

Or alternatively, hypothetically, just maybe, is the very question of "bad things happening" fatally flawed? Perhaps the presumption that bad things even happen misses the mark. Which would mean that bad things *don't* happen. That nothing is pointless. That "unexpected" simply means serendipitous, not random.

Well, *wouldn't this make sense?* Wouldn't you expect that in *the* Kingdom, the Home of the Divine, given the splendor and order you see everywhere, there would be valuable meaning and a constructive purpose behind all occurrences? Doesn't this make sense?! If not for the existence of massive contradictory evidence, would you have expected *any* nastiness in "God's kitchen"? *No f-in' way!* Right?

This would make sense! That your glorious bastion of perfection, your floating emerald nestled in the Milky Way galaxy, *ought to be* a turnkey, good-to-go Garden of Eden from day one, forever and ever? *This makes sense!* Where everything hummed, sparkled, and glowed; purred, wagged, and nuzzled; loved, was lovable, and served? Isn't that what you'd expect from the Divine? *Hallelujah!*

With so much now making sense, let's go to that seemingly contradictory evidence for a closer look.

WATER RISES TO ITS OWN LEVEL

Surely by now you're on board with the notion that thoughts become things. Maybe not convinced of its pervasive absoluteness, but you're getting there.

You also don't have to be a tie-dye-wearing hippie to get what's meant by someone's "energetic vibration": that if they think and feel warm and fuzzy, they'll "vibrate" and thus attract warm and fuzzy—situations, people, whatever. If they think and feel negative and angry, they will "vibrate" negative and angry, and thus similarly attract such. Right? You might also equate one's "vibe" with his combined thoughts, beliefs, and expectations (usually I just say thoughts) with regard to a particular subject.

I think you see where this is going—positive thoughts create positive manifestations, just as negative thoughts create negative ones—and I think you're guessing that I'm about to tell you that this, and therefore all of life, is fair. Right-o. Which some may think is an overly sweeping declaration, especially because in the to'ing and fro'ing of the world, it's easy to miss *how* this works.

Case Study #1

So take the gloriously positive person whose financial energetic vibration roughly corresponds to having

$30,000 net worth, and for convenience's sake, let's say that this, therefore, is the cash he usually has in his savings account. This is a very simplistic example for illustrative purposes. In actuality, our vibes aren't ever so exacting; they fluctuate constantly, though usually minutely, reflecting changes in our worldview, our priorities, our beliefs, and our reaction to the economy, trends, and a kaleidoscope of other shifting criteria. And keep in mind that our financial vibe is probably never really a number we think of but the convergence of all of our thoughts that directly and indirectly lead to our financial net worth—numerical, material, spiritual, worthiness, and so on.

With a vibe pegged at $30,000, whatever else his thoughts permit in his life, financially speaking he will eventually arrive at, and always return to, a savings account of $30,000. This is accomplished the way all manifestations come to pass, through a seamless, often imperceptible shifting of circumstances that keep his balance at $30,000.

Now if this same person also believes he is vulnerable to circumstances, life is hard, and it's tough to get ahead, he may thereby unwittingly manifest a leaky roof on his home that costs $12,000 to repair. Over time, in alignment with his other beliefs about the speed of accumulating wealth and its opportunity to find him, if his vibe remains at $30,000, the $12,000 will return to him. Perhaps as a gift from someone, an income tax refund, work bonuses, commission checks, a scratch-off lottery win, or most commonly, through a combination of several lesser amounts arriving in a variety of ways. To him, the repair bill and the subsequent gradual replenishment will seem completely unrelated yet his thoughts, his vibe, will have directly led to both.

It works the same in reverse. If there's an unexpected windfall of money—for example, an additional $25,000 made possible by other *fleeting* beliefs and actions, maybe an inheritance check—yet his overall vibe remains at $30,000, the windfall will eventually be eroded through a series of expenditures, his generosity, repairs, bad habits, so-called mistakes, or whatever else fits within his worldview, leaving him back at $30,000.

Nothing bad, and nothing good, has happened. Just thoughts becoming things under the guise of shifting circumstances brought about by his energetic vibe.

The Math (Beliefs) Behind Every Manifestation

This extremely simplistic monetary example helps you quantitatively understand the processes involved in creating change, yet the process of *vibe + action = life experiences* pervades and rules every experience of every single life within the jungles.

Health, enlightenment, confidence, motivation, creativity, energy levels, weight loss/gain, friendships, partners, peace, pain, business, play, even photo-geniality! Everything, everything, everything, everything, everything, *everything*. While you have natural-born default levels of love, joy, health, and all things good, you can actually override them with beliefs that may be in contradiction. Your beliefs spin off *thoughts* in their likeness, and then as you live your life (that is, take action) those thoughts whirl around, becoming the things of your experience. Your energetic vibration is powerful *because* it inspires your thoughts that then become things:

Confluence of beliefs ➔ Energetic vibe ➔ *Thoughts and expectations* ➔ Action ➔ Coincidences, accidents, serendipities ➔ Reaction ➔ *Manifestation matching earlier thoughts and expectations* ➔ (*REPEAT* as evolving beliefs stream and blend to create a corresponding worldview with reinforced beliefs)

Or, simpler:

Beliefs ➔ Vibe ➔ Thoughts ➔ Action ➔ Circumstances ➔ Things

Or, vastly simplified:

Thoughts Become Things

RHYMES AND REASONS

Such is the nature of beliefs: as they inspire or shut down the wondering imagination (the thoughts) of their believer, so do they allow or prevent new worlds' being born.

It's completely irrelevant *why* you believe what you believe, however logical or illogical it may be, prudent or reckless, conservative or aggressive, self-serving or altruistic; that you do believe is sufficient for manifestation. Of course, as I mentioned earlier, there's a very loose need that the beliefs be in sync with the prevailing mass beliefs of the time, but for your presence here and now, this pretty much means they're already *your* beliefs, too (see Chapter 3, "We were ready").

All that matters is that the belief is there (creating the vibe), that it's not contradicted by other beliefs, known or unknown, and that the believer is showing up in the world (physically taking action), thereby available to an inconceivably vast network of potential coincidences, accidents, and serendipities. Plus, given your inclination to succeed and your default settings of joy, health, clarity, friends, abundance, and all other good things, you needn't overly fret or worry that you're fretting and worrying—that's normal! Just do what you can with what you have from where you are, while understanding the truth about your reality and your divine heritage, and you'll quickly become unstoppable. Not that there won't continue to be challenges, but more and more they'll be understood as gifts that ultimately reveal previously unrecognized shortcuts forward.

> You needn't overly fret or worry that you're fretting and worrying—that's normal!

It may seem at times that your efforts are futile, yet it takes time for the pendulum to swing. And it always swings. In the very unlikely event that circumstances prevent it from swinging back in one lifetime, as long as the energy remains, the results will appear in the next: the *phenomenon* of karma. For example, consider the good Samaritan who lives in a tidy little house with a manicured yard, polite and friendly, who often picks up other people's accidental garbage as it blows across parking lots or litters his neighborhood. Whether or not he begins to experience and be drawn to like-minded do-gooders in that lifetime, his unchanging vibe *will* draw him toward such people, communities, and worlds in subsequent lifetimes.

Similarly, the military combatant who believes that people are brutal, violent, and evil; that she lives in a kill-or-be-killed world; and that violence can be justifiable when one's ideals are superior to another's will continue to be drawn to such people, communities, and worlds in her future incarnations until she changes her thinking. Her vibe will create circumstances that will pit her against (draw her to) people who think like she does, thoroughly and incontestably confirming her beliefs. Such cycles would repeat eternally *were it not for your inherent goodness,* likelihood of success, and default settings previously named, all of which are sufficient to right any listing ship, ultimately and naturally bringing everyone back into the fold of truth.

In the meantime, it may also seem as if others can add to or take from what you have and who you are, yet at the end of every "day," what you have and who you are is entirely a function of *your* thoughts, beliefs, and expectations. This is the name of the game in time and space, where you draw from the ether whatever matches your own groovy (or goopy) vibe. It's just that until now, when there have been unpleasant serendipities and coincidences—really just positioning you for future manifestation of what you've been "putting out there"—such events and those involved have been seen outside the context of the overall creation, so they've been termed "bad."

Too easy? Baby cake examples? More's coming.

You Happen to Life

To create a physical world that corresponds to all the vibes you possess, *life happens.* What's critical right now is your understanding that your vibes come first.

Actually, it's more accurate to say that *you happen to life* and then life responds. *You* came first, remember?

You are the reason for the jungles and you're the reason the sun continues to rise each day. You are the Creator. Not the only Creator, but the epicenter of the energy that brings about your life's manifestations. Life, incidentally, is not 10 percent what you make it and 90 percent how you take it! It's 100 percent what you make it.

Sure, you're just waking up, so there'll be surprises along the way, surprises *you* unknowingly created. And in such cases, by all means roll with them. Realize that the hows and whys will all make sense soon enough. Don't jump to conclusions when something surprises you, for better or worse, whether it's a diagnosis or a business proposal. It *is* important that you "take it" well, but not with the view that you are powerless before it. Thinking so *makes you so.* You could not be more powerful than you already are. Yet if you think:

- ☀ That life is happening to you,
- ☀ That unfortunate, random things happen for no reason or purpose,
- ☀ That anyone might end up a victim, and
- ☀ That other people are the cause of your experiences,

then you may as well believe that your hallowed jungles are the random chance by-product of space dust that collided a trillion years ago, fortuitously landing in a warm body of water only to beat all odds and grow gills, fins, and intelligence sufficient to evolve into walking upon the earth, standing upright, and finally, wearing high heels!

Instead, if you embrace the truth:

❀ You happen to life,

❀ Everything happens for a reason,

❀ You are untouchable by others, and

❀ You are the Creator of your experiences,

then you understand how life works, you are assured of your inclination to succeed, and whenever the unexpected happens you simply take it in stride, knowing that sometimes in life you must take one step back to take many more forward.

THE BEST NEWS

So, forgetting how things appear—since appearances are the product of thoughts, beliefs, and vibes—the person who comes into a million dollars, or loses it, does so entirely on his own as the outer world is ultimately mirrored by his inner world. He will then keep that money, grow it, or lose it based on the energetic financial vibe he maintains. Every stroke of luck, however good or bad, every fortune or misfortune, every twist and turn in the plot of his life, *no matter who else* was involved and no matter what role they played, is self-created. Finally knowing this, anyone can deliberately change his "luck"!

> **Life is not 10 percent what you make it and 90 percent how you take it! It's 100 percent what you make it.**

Case Study #2

We'll use another financial hypothetical, again for simplistic, quantitative illustration purposes, although it works exactly the same for love, health, happiness, or whatever your heart now desires. Take an entrepreneurial tycoon with a net worth (financial vibe) of $1 million who one year, because of a few uncharacteristically optimistic thoughts, overshot her goals and projections and increased her net worth to $1.7 million. *If her vibe remained unchanged at $1 million,* the $700,000 surplus will eventually "vanish." In this make-believe example, let's say the surplus is "taken" in a subsequent investment, naïvely entered into under fraudulent pretenses—which, of course, could only happen if this was *consistent with her other life vibes.* Even though there was an indisputable "bad guy," a crook in the mix, the true cause of the decrease in her worth would be her lower vibe, *not the "bad guy"!* The "victim" and "thief" attracted each other because they each believed in and needed the other to achieve manifestations that matched their corresponding vibes.

To flip the equation, this is also how *every* fortune was made and how every wonderful thing has ever happened to anyone. First, there's someone who believes, "It could happen to me," "I'm smart enough," "I deserve it," "God favors me," "I've paid my dues," "My tea leaves told me I'd be rich" . . . again, the rationale is irrelevant. Second, the one who so believes—not just claims to believe but *truly believes*—without contradiction *and who physically shows up regularly* will legitimately, or illegitimately, according to her own beliefs, amass a fortune.

Galling, huh? At least at first, anyway. Gone are all excuses, forevermore. Yet empowering, too! Thrilling!

Fantastic! What could possibly be better? What could possibly be easier? Don't like your lot in life? *Change it!* Think it, feel it, expect it, act as if, show up, and prepare to be astounded.

Though none of this, as I stated previously, excuses the poor behavior of the "bad guy," nor does it mean he shouldn't be criminally dealt with. Nor should such a swindle be viewed as deserved or the "victim" considered at fault, as you will soon read.

No Matter How Ugly

Depending on where your creations have taken you so far in this lifetime, these ideas may be insulting or painful at first, yet the truth is your salvation. It will restore your power and give you renewed hope. And please consider: this book is merely the messenger. As a doctor who explains AIDS does not justify it, endorse it, or deny that it's a hideous disease, she merely explains it, so are these merely descriptions of the unbending, nonjudgmental logistics behind all time-space creations. There's also no such thing as an innocent villain, and I'll reiterate that it is absolutely not okay that they violate others, no matter how the stage was set. Nevertheless, the implications of how life truly unfolds are absolutely staggering—and diametrically opposed to the "old" worldview virtually everyone who's ever lived has had.

It's fantastically easier, and politically preferable, to believe there are evil people doing evil things and that they will be punished in hell for eternity by the devil who goaded them on in the first place. It's also far easier to believe that you have been a victim of other people who took advantage of you than a victim of your own naïveté or curiosity. At least it used to be easier to believe such explanations, except that now you're waking up and there's pretty much no going back.

There are no evil people, just lost people who do evil things. There are also sick people. Warped people. Deranged people. Lots of different people, yet all of them once set out just like you did, a "God Particle," to find their way through the jungles of time and space. Every single one of them of good intent yet some so fundamentally confused or new to time and space that they behave horrifically. The difference between you and them might boil down to you having lived thousands or tens of thousands more lifetimes, whereas they may be true babes, utterly terrified, with no defense mechanisms developed yet but hatred, anger, contempt, manipulation, coercion, and violence. It's not as if in life, between two people, all other things remain equal. Nothing else is ever equal.

More than everyone else, even, those who are lost need love. Help. Guidance. Patience. Yet very likely, if they've strayed too far from truth, this lifetime will not nearly be long enough for them to find balance and clarity. They won't be safe, either for themselves or for others who similarly believe the world is an evil place. They'll need rehabilitation, ideally in a nurturing, supportive environment, yet if society *believes* this is out of reach, emotionally or financially, prisons and institutions will have to suffice.

Suffer the Little Children

No matter how few lifetimes one has had in the jungles, all of us are ancient gladiators of love and joy.

Similarly, no matter people's physical age, or the age of a young child or infant in the world, they're *ancient*. And the reasons for suffering are innumerable.

When horrible things happen to the most innocent of lives,

- ☀ Perhaps, just maybe, it's because an ancient gladiator carried over unfinished business from a prior life . . . or

- ☀ Perhaps she placed herself on a certain "stage" around certain people so that others wouldn't have to . . . or

- ☀ Maybe there was initially an opportunity to prevent the violation, if she chose to be involved, that didn't ultimately "play out". . . or

- ☀ Maybe, however brief her present lifetime, she had already achieved what she was there for, and its sad ending played a much smaller role for her than it did for her survivors, while enabling them to live through their own chosen lessons . . . or

- ☀ Perhaps there were multiple reasons for the violation, one of which was getting the attention of others—family members, loved ones, a nation, or the entire world—so that similar atrocities might be exposed and ended.

In which case, wouldn't the "victim" actually be a mighty hero?

Please be patient; these are massively new ideas given the times. There's still more to come that will help give you a handle on these radical concepts. Meanwhile, there's no question that hideous and ugly things happen in time and space, although if you look to understand them with your eyes alone, you will not see all. Open your heart and your mind, for again, even as circumstances may indeed be wildly unfair, when you see them in their greater context you'll find that intention, healing, order, and love were present all along.

> Now you're waking up and there's pretty much no going back.

Fault and Blame (More "Blame the Victim"?)

"So those who trip and stumble or who are hurt and 'victimized' by others are to blame for what they supposedly brought upon themselves?!"

Again we meet the "blame the victim" syndrome so commonly hurled about when truth is revealed to eyes that have been closed too long. Yet those three words presume things that don't apply. Fault and blame don't fit into the equation of understanding that you're an eternal Creator who chose to enroll in a Creator's school.

Consider an infant learning to take her very first steps. As you might expect, she trips and falls. Is she to blame? Is it her fault? You certainly could say yes to both, but would you? Do they capture the essence of what's happening? Or are they unnecessarily negative and inappropriate? More, don't such words characterize the occurrence as history instead of as a process; as a destination, not a journey?

How about "Look! Our baby's learning to walk! She's taken her first step!" No implication of wrong there. You wouldn't blame her for her wobble and fall. This is more than a "glass half full or half empty" analysis; your new perspective recognizes there's a process under way, learning to walk, that's far bigger than any single step or slip within it. A process that will elevate the initiate into new realms of mobility, adventure, and learning. Indeed, the glass is completely full: half water and half air.

Life in the jungles is such a process, one leading to adventure and growth so spectacular that it can't even be fathomed from within the illusions. Yet life in the jungles is sufficient unto itself, and however great the promises are of adventures in wait, the present moment alone is grand enough for virtually anyone to begin, at once, having more fun and living a happier life. You're enrolled in a Creator's school, but far from being the Harvard of the Universe, it's more like kindergarten— with giggling friends, daily field trips, and bright stars awarded for just showing up. Don't focus on the ugly, but the beauty; not on what's hard or complicated, but what's easy and fun. Rainbows, butterflies, and falling snow. Kindness, hugs, and kisses. Dolphins, lavender, and Beethoven. Winks, confidence, and holding hands. Skipping, jumping, and playing. Mentors, friends, and helpers. Swimming, splashing, and sand. Romance, tenderness, and presents.

Is Life Fair?

Life is like a nighttime dream. You create it for a reason—lessons and adventure—and it has meaning, order, and purpose, yet you forget that you're creating it because only by (fleetingly) believing it's real can you learn its lessons and secrets. All is well. And once the dream is over, it'll make perfect sense. You'll see it balances itself on the fly. Don't let the linear time sequences or rigid props deceive you; sequences follow intention, shapes shift when you blink, and pasts are remade in each moment. No, you'll never be able to wrap your brain around all of this, but you don't have to in order to sense what's going on. To stop playing the victim, bust a move, and soar.

Your physical senses see virtually nothing of the magic, the love, or the reasons for the miracles involved in every moment you live. Yet you have other faculties at your disposal. You have inner senses: intellect, intuition, and feelings. Use them to peel away the lies. Discover the truths that will set you free and give you wings, even as you linger upon the earth for just a little while longer, where:

1. It doesn't matter where you've been—it will serve you,

2. It doesn't even matter where you now are, because where you are is never who you are, and

3. You can, starting today, with new thoughts, words and actions, create a new vibe that will begin orchestrating your own "luck, accidents, and serendipities" to blast forward, higher, richer, and happier— yee-ha!

Actually, dear heart, *life is not fair*—the cards are incredibly stacked in your favor.

From a Dearly Departed

Dear Lottery Officials:

Sorry about all the nasty-grams I sent you; I think one a day for a while there.

I get it. Nothing was rigged. I wasn't unlucky. And racism was clearly not a factor.

Thoughts become things. Emotions rule. Their intensity and one's expectations are the deciding factors that draw from the possibilities life's next set of props and events. It doesn't matter how many tickets someone buys unless it increases their own expectations of a win. Statistics only measure the past, not the future. And whatever's necessary to live the life one's imagined will be arranged through the most uncanny wins, losses, inspiration, hesitation, best friends, and enemies required to live in a corresponding physical world.

Oh, I believed I could win, all right. I wouldn't have bought the tickets if I hadn't! And I visualized so often, usually before falling asleep at night, that worlds were born. But now I see that sometimes the difference between have and have not is the other beliefs we don't acknowledge having. Like me thinking the world was unfair, that money was unspiritual (while I otherwise strived to be spiritual in spite of my nasty-grams), that life was a test, that God decided who would get what, that I didn't deserve to win or to have money or to be happy . . .

Funny, now, how from here I see money everywhere in time and space. Everyone has it. I even had it, yet by focusing on all that I did not have, I felt poor. And feelings of anything tend to perpetuate themselves while rearranging our lives to match those feelings. It's a wonder that I managed to keep anything of value, although the fact that I did probably means I was also more positive than I might now be giving myself credit for.

From here I can't help but notice all the folks attracting wealth into their lives by doing the simplest of things . . . like working a job! Seriously? Which, while I was alive, would have been the last place I would have sought it. Whether they work for themselves or someone else doesn't matter. "Work," hands down, is the fastest and easiest way to open the financial floodgates. Who knew? Working smart, asking questions, showing up early, staying late, and in spite of appearances dwelling upon what's right, who you already are, and all you already have and have done. Not just at big fancy jobs with long fancy titles and lots of education; the people who typically earn the most have neither. Go ahead, look around you and see if this isn't still true.

Funny how I and so many others used to think the easiest and fastest trick to make money was to win it when there are so many easier and faster tricks—like, just live your life and have fun! Fun! Everyone is a money magnet when they're happy. Trying to win your fortune as if it were the only way to hit it rich is a fast track to boredom and misery, even if you do somehow win it.

Being happy makes you a magnet for everything else, too. In fact, from here we can see that the truly happy people are those who are led by their own joy and therefore automatically have dreams they physically dance with, moving and grooving in the world every day. They don't even need to think of money to have money, health to have health, friends to have friends, clarity to have clarity, opportunity to have opportunities . . . *everything* is drawn to them because the happiness they feel perpetuates itself—not as in "happy for no reason" but as in "happy for lots of great reasons," material and ethereal. Their vibe summons circumstances, new friends, money, confidence, inspiration, *and all things necessary to continue being happy* as they define happy. Sure, thoughts become things, but thoughts of happiness become all things good, which is what true happiness implies. Whoa! Lottery People! This is huge. Life isn't just fair, it's more than fair, an unending banquet for those who live in truth.

Nothing is as it appears in time and space, particularly for those in a hurry. Invariably, the shortcut will turn out to be the long way and the easy way will turn out to be the hard way, while what seem to be the slow and hard ways are neither. From now on I'll choose the "happy way" and then time won't matter.

Well, you taught me a lot, Lottery Officials. A whole lot. Def feeling like a winner right now. And again, I hope my early letters didn't dampen your spirit, just as much as I hope this letter doesn't hurt your sales.

Going *BIG!*

Jethro

SEE MORE, HEAL FASTER, SLEEP BETTER

There's little rest for the weary, especially those who suffer from their past or who feel the pain of others hurting around the world. These words are not meant to negate or minimize their experience, only to offer insight

so you better understand it as you simultaneously pro-
vide comfort and move to limit possibilities for future
manifestations of pain.

See more. Look with understanding. Help others
regain use of their power. Help yourself do the same.
Life is waiting. You are blessed. Tame the jungles and
you will find a world eager to fill your every cup, coffer,
and bathtub.

Speaking of tame jungles, we have them here. And
would you ever guess who the kings and queens are
now? Read on.

CHAPTER 9

YOUR "OLD" PETS ARE AS CRAZY AS EVER.

Would you have thought less?

If things like cancer actually impart life-changing gifts, if setbacks are really setups for greatness, and if even "death" is actually a rendezvous point for loved ones, surely you'd guess that the Divine's idea for its own furry companions would be no less stunning—God particles themselves, lit up in love, best friends for life and beyond?

Yes, and more. Not only are you loved through the packages and bundles that are Fido and Fifi, but their presence in your life is just one more invitation for you to love as you could not have loved otherwise, even as they teach you lessons of compassion, tolerance, patience, or whatever else you stand in need of. Not that they're there to test you, but as you create your own tests through misunderstandings, these friends can help you weather the storm.

Losses are only devastating when you think they're permanent. They never are.

Clever are the ways of the Divine. Not in orchestrating the twists and turns of your life, as is usually implied—*you alone do that*—but in crafting such jungles where everything has depth and meaning and everything makes you, and thereby Itself, more. Including the pets you fall in love with.

It's no wonder, then, that immersed in the illusions as you are, when you see your young companion's life slip away you feel devastation, grief, and a profound sense of loss. God has come and gone from your life, or so it would seem. Yet losses are only devastating when you think they're permanent. They never are. Your loved ones, furry and otherwise, are here. As happy as they have ever been. And you will be together again, only to fall even deeper in love. Nothing has been lost, only gained, you will see—and this, too, the "dead" long to tell you.

ANIMAL CONSCIOUSNESS

The main difference between animal consciousness and your own is that animals don't possess your self-reflective abilities. They're not as aware of themselves as you are of yourself, which is why they're generally nonexpectant and nonjudgmental. Which, in turn, means they're completely unconcerned with the past and the future, and this in turn allows them to focus almost exclusively in the present. Their instincts alone are sufficient to guide them into the wisest behavior to ensure their survival. Otherwise, they love, fear, trust, resent, guard, discard, protect, envy, obey, and genuinely feel many of the very same emotions you feel, for the very same reasons you feel them—although usually in healthier, more immediate doses.

Yet for all their focus in the moment, they're not Creators as people are; their thoughts do not become things. They are reactors to the world, not projectors of it. They're also pure God, of God, by God, yet they exist:

1. To perceive, experience, and revel in life's magic and

2. To create new dimensions of learning for those who do have self-reflective abilities— like you.

They achieve this by creatively living in the moment, following impulses, urges, and their innate desire to play and explore. Additionally, their mere presence makes the world more interesting, diverse, fun, and interactive for the self-reflectors while balancing ecosystems, adding to the believability of time and space, and helping self-reflectors not self-reflect too much.

Generally, animal consciousness *not* touched by a relationship with a self-reflector does not reincarnate, as these animals don't have any forward-leaning vision and thus no unfinished business. They do not, however, cease to exist, dissolving back into the Divine. Remember, that could only happen if time were absolute. Time is an illusion. In ways you cannot comprehend from within it, once any being or God particle exists, it does so eternally in an ever-evolving "now."

Pet Consciousness

Pet consciousness is like animal consciousness—pure God, "alive" and responding to everything—yet is changed by the personality and love of the pet's owner.

Animals absorb and react to the energy of those they live with. Expectations are mildly aroused, sufficient to change their spiritual evolution. Plus, the projection of human qualities upon them by their owners *instills such qualities*. And as reactors, they mirror the energies they receive. Richer personalities thus develop, and they become forward-seeing, not as self-reflectors but able to continue exploring and expanding at new levels.

In any household with pets, the animals rise to meet the expectations imposed upon them (for example, to behave or misbehave, to nurture or protect) while also reflecting the patience, compassion, exuberance, anger, openness, and shyness of those around them. Owners can always find "themselves" in their pets.

Loved pets not only evolve in an eternal "now" like all animals, but the personalities they develop create will, intention, and desire sufficient to generate unfinished business and a return to a subsequent time and space incarnation, whether with the same owners or new ones. The choice of whom to return with is left to all involved.

WHO RESCUED WHOM

As with all time-space connections, there's always groundwork that comes first. A commingling of thoughts, expectations, and desires (aka beliefs or vibe) in the unseen—including the animal's—precedes any physical-world circumstances that lead to meet-ups. And like all manifestations, this is exactly how you came to meet and adopt your furry friends, assuming you have such, or perhaps how they came to meet and adopt you.

Whether first-time connections or the continuation of unfinished business, serendipities lead to "accidents and coincidences" that enable the most authentic, spontaneous, and believably real events to transpire, bringing together the loving parties.

Like attracts like. Thoughts, people, animals, pets. And given that there are always multiple choices and probabilities in your world of illusions for the manifestation to answer every need, that you "found" who you "found" and that they "found" you has deep meaning and occurs with flawless precision. The world would not and could not have proceeded even one more day on the path it was on until each of you was present for the other, to be shaped by each other's love, to learn by each other's example, to teach, to laugh, and to heal.

PLANT CONSCIOUSNESS

You're going to ask, so yeah, plants have consciousness. Not like the living or the "dead" or animals or pets, yet they're aware, they're intelligent, and they yearn to expand. They're simple. They're joyful. They are pure God. And they *respond* to their environment—to sunlight, water, birds, bees, and all other forms of consciousness that share their time and space. They especially respond to your expectations and feelings, far more than they do to your voice. Speak to your plants expecting them to positively respond and they will, not because you spoke to them but because of the energy, intentions, and expectations that sent your words forth.

Like animals and pets, plants understand that their existence is paramount to the survival of life—for everything to exist within the jungles—and to the earth herself. They know that to exist is to serve. Yet surviving is not their goal; it's just a first step. Thriving is the goal for every form and expression of life. When one species thrives, growing healthy and strong, all are aided. And all life senses this, with the exception of most humans, given the early stage of human development.

Ours is the species that can most affect other species.

Yet while there's a universal recognition of the symbiosis at play in time and space in which each particle, cell, or species is serving the greater good of the whole through its mere existence, all understand and honor their sacred, irreplaceable individuality. They understand that it's their unique expression as much as their contribution to the whole that adds to and expands the very definition of All That Is—the very reason for their being.

Dolphins and Whales

More than pets, loved by humans or not, there are other species on earth with such profound intellectual, emotional, and self-reflective abilities that the variety of adventures and discoveries that are possible for them can't be contained in one mere lifetime. So in the same way humans reincarnate (which was kind of, sort of), so do dolphins, whales, and very likely other species.

In this passage, the dead would love to be more precise, but they're only dead; they're not all-knowing. Perhaps one day *The Top Ten Things All-Knowing Beings Want to Tell YOU* will be written, *yet you'd hardly need to read it to begin immediately respecting and revering all life,* reincarnational or otherwise. Besides, apart from it being a fascinating question, it doesn't matter whether or not elephants, octopuses, or ravens reincarnate. What matters is your life now. Your challenges, your discoveries, your thriving, all of which you're most capable of without further animal studies. The life of every creature, each being of and for God, is obviously known and understood by God, serving its purpose, fulfilling its role. And when it's relevant, no doubt you will share in this knowing.

As for dolphins and whales, as with humans, some are baby souls while others are experienced and wiser. Some have found that love and compassion are the only choices that will achieve lasting joy and fulfillment, and others are still finding their way through experimentations in anger and other shortsighted behaviors. They communicate as much telepathically (as do thousands of the earth's species, unbeknownst to you) as they do audibly and behaviorally. Expression, cooperation, and service could be named as their ultimate reasons for being, just as they could for you, with each equally important, although patience, tolerance, and other lessons are theirs as well.

They are love-beings, as you are a love-being. Unlike plants, other animals, and pets, however, they have creative will, intentions, and time-forward vision, all of which radically increases future possibilities and probabilities for their spiritual evolution. They are truly your brothers from different mothers, fully fledged God particles, Mini-Me's of the Divine.

DOMINION OVER ALL THINGS

By the way, "dominion over all things," as is quoted from the Bible so often throughout much of the world, has been grossly misinterpreted to mean "power over all things" or "do whatever you want to all things." As most holy books' original meanings have been lost in translation, this phrase has been misused to such a degree that many casually believe that the very reason fowl, cattle, and fish exist is for you to eat them.

You may do so. You have free will. You have the ability. You will not be judged either way. But just because you *can* do something doesn't mean you're *supposed* to do it.

Again, with great power comes great responsibility. Being the only (known) land-dwelling species on the planet bestowed with time-forward thinking and thumbs, humans are the species that can most affect other species. We, therefore, have *the greatest responsibility over all things.* As we've multiplied into the billions, our presence is so monumentally sweeping that we have no choice but to consider other species when we make decisions that will affect them. We have, therefore, unintentionally become the de facto *guardian over all things,* including our precious planet herself. We're beginning to clearly see the power we have over our environment, food supplies, and natural resources, and as the pendulum swings it's now within our reach to see our responsibilities as well. Again, this awakening is what the 2012 buzz was all about: acceptance of, versus resistance to, our stewardship role, *individually and collectively.*

By the way, since dominion over "all things," which would obviously include trees, boulders, and hillsides, clearly does not mean eating "all things," why do you think it might mean this for the animals? Because they're edible? So are bugs, grass, and people. Because your ancestors ate them? They were mostly baby souls. Because you breed and sustain them? You do that for your children. Plus, aren't there many obvious reasons for the existence of animals other than your nourishment? Aren't there obvious resource costs and sacrifices associated with converting them into food, financially and environmentally, that do not present themselves when growing a nonanimal diet? And isn't there an enormous diversity of other foods that have long been scientifically proven to be equally nourishing?

You may have already surmised by now that the animals in question knew the probabilities for their being consumed as food that they were getting themselves into. Indeed they did. But so do *people* know the probabilities of possible violations before choosing a lifetime, and they choose to come anyway, which by no means excuses any violations that may later follow.

If you're curious, the solution that seems most fitting to resolve an "omnivore's dilemma" is to ask yourself before any meal, "Are the meat options before me necessary for my *survival* or just more convenient than other foods?" No doubt, if you find yourself starving to death, even the animals you eat would celebrate that their life might extend yours. Otherwise, however, you might reconsider your options to be more win-win for the other species that equally crave the experience called "life on earth."

ALIEN CONSCIOUSNESS

Yes, from other planets. They're real. Some of us are their descendants; some of them are our descendants. The lines of origin are blurry and unimportant. Besides, any objective definitions of source depend on the "lies" of time and space, so to debate which came first, the chicken or the egg, is always futile.

Simply know: you are not alone, you live in a loving Universe, nothing is by chance, everyone is doing their best (as they then define it), thoughtful cooperation is essential whenever two or more share "space" (which would then always be of their co-creation), and accepting personal responsibility for everything you experience is critical to ultimately discovering your power, individually, collectively, and "intergalactically."

MOTHER EARTH

A big rock? A figment of your imagination? Both. But then, both rocks and imagination are more than you've ever thought they might be.

To cut to the chase, earth also has a consciousness. That you think of it, talk to it, have expectations of it, *adds* to its consciousness. Yet it was living and breathing long "before" you physically appeared—although, significantly, so that you *could* physically appear.

Think of your own body. What's it made of? Whirling electrons and protons, atoms, molecules, and chemical collections; tissues, bones, and organs; extremities, torso, and head. Then ask yourself where "you" reside within this masterpiece. Does the conscious, thinking you live in the head? Somewhere in the brain—left lobe, right lobe? The heart or the solar plexus?

The thinking you, *as you have sensed,* is not a product of your brain; it is channeled by your brain. It does not physically reside in your body. *You know that.* Even as you peer at the world *through* your eyes, not *from* your eyes, your essence transcends the illusions. Your physical body is the portal of your spirit, the God fragment that you are, through which you physically experience and shape the world you create. Yet as with all consciousness, it also takes on its own awareness independent of yours; it exists to serve, yet it will have its own experiences and expansion.

It's the same for Mother Earth. She is more than a collection of liquids, gases, and rocks; deserts, oceans, and mountains; core, crust, and mantle, although physically she is all of these things. She exists so you and all of her life-forms can exist, yet in "being," she becomes her own life-form with her own consciousness that is greater than the sum of the roles she fulfills. She is alive, yet her spiritual center is not located in any place, neither in the northern nor the southern hemisphere. Like yours, the body of the earth is the portal through which "her" spirit emerges with intention, purpose, and desire. She does not, therefore, exist only existentially for your benefit but as a flowing, moving, "alive," intelligent energy, independent of, yet intertwined with, the consciousness of all the beings she supports, co-creating and re-creating herself in every moment.

Your pets once existed for you; now they exist because of you.

She knows you are just learning of your responsibilities. She is patient. She can adapt and compensate, and she has. And now, as you've already begun to do, it's your turn to do the same.

You'll Meet Again

There's a reason and rhyme to all that happens, including the presence of those beings in your life who love you, no matter the species.

Your furry friends, former and present, are your playmates and teachers and are one of the many ways you can say that "God" reaches deep into your physical corner of creation to open your heart and mind. They are angels with paws, beaks, gills, and tails. Your pets once existed for you; now they exist because of you. That you loved them raised their vibration, and even as you read these words, their spirit soars and lives on. The funny ways and silly habits that endeared them to you are their trademarks, bringing laughter and smiles wherever they continue to go, as well as an extra special gift to those so in need . . . a little bit of you. Your compassion and love are now part of them and will be forever more. They couldn't be prouder, happier, or more eager to lick your face again, wag their tails, purr their little hearts out in your warm lap. Yet they're wise enough to know of that day's inevitability, as are you. In the meantime, they play, heal others, expand, and become more as they patiently await your homecoming, which is exactly what they wish for you to know . . . and do.

From a Dearly Departed

Dear Mom—

You will *never* guess where I am . . .

The forest!

And you'll never guess what color everything is . . .

Green!

Life is amazing here—things to chase, streams to swim in, nastiness to roll in . . . The occasional lost camper, who always thinks that he's found me and that I needed rescuing. Whatever. I play along, teach them to throw, to trust, and to love again. Like we do on earth.

You'd be surprised at how many people here still need us. Seriously. Remember how I taught you to stop feeling sorry for yourself? That comes in handy here. And remember when I helped you forget your boyfriends? To believe in yourself? Take better care of yourself? Those were my best tricks and I use them here too.

How are you? Are you getting out of bed on time without me? Do you still laugh out loud for no reason?

I hope you don't mind how happy I am. I hope you're not jealous. Some moms are. Or they miss their pets so much that their pets can't move on. Of course, their pets don't mind—they love their moms more than life itself. But if their moms are sad, then they're sad. And why be sad when everything's so great? When every good-bye guarantees a future "Who's a good boy?" When there are so many who now need you, furry and human, in their presence? So many . . .

Besides, how can you miss someone who's with you?

Why cry for what seems lost when there's still so much to find?

Why let grief for what "is not" blind you to what "still is and must always be"?

Why see life with only your eyes, when your heart has double-secret, interdimensional, X-ray vision?

Unless, of course, you don't know any better.

Mom, you gave me my eyes, my heart, and my love for life. *Squirrel!!!!* Without you I could not have carried on here in the unseen as I have. You don't know it yet, but what we shared has rocked the world—not just ours, but the entire world, everyone's world. Now it's my turn to give back to you, so please hear what I'm saying: Do not think I'm lost, because of you I was found. Don't think my life is over, instead it has just begun. And do not regret what we didn't do, where we didn't go, or what we didn't have, to know you was more than I even knew to hope for. That we spent so much of my life together . . . you can't even begin to understand my gratitude.

Please celebrate every day, enjoy every moment, and love, love, love everything, everyone, every how and every way, just as you so unconditionally loved me.

I'm here for you, Mom. The fact that I'm happy doesn't mean I'm not waiting. You were the best part of my life. I'll never wander farther than your thoughts can reach. And I'll be the first to welcome you home . . .

"Who let the dogs out?"

Brutus

P.S. And guess what else! Remember the shiny gold bangle you hid for me in plain view on the couch? It's in the yard, under the stairs—not so chewy or squeaky. Besides, it made you think too much of Jim, and I wanted you to be there for Josh. You'll be meeting him once you start getting out more. Hubba hubba!

Every Sparrow

The dead want you to know that nothing and no one is left behind, ever. There are no bad dogs. Every cat gets more lives. And you can rest assured of more sloppy kisses, licks, and chirps in the next world, so great is the love behind creation.

Life really is all about love, but not just the kind you feel for those who love you. A much bigger love. Which is next and last on this top ten list.

CHAPTER 10

LOVE IS THE WAY; TRUTH IS THE PATH.

No one knows how it all began, not even the dead, but everyone knows that it did.

Actually, no one knows much of anything at all, except:

1. Everything is God,

2. Thoughts become things, and

3. Love is all.

Concerning love: not the kind that's given or received by others. Although beautiful, that kind of love is triggered by conditions. It's an emotion that requires stimulus and reason.

Instead, a love:

❋ That's always, everywhere on,

❋ With a benevolence that does not need approval or judgment to be shared,

❋ Bearing gifts that do not need to be earned or deserved, and

❋ Consisting of a uniting, healing, intelligent superjoy.

Yet this is a love that often blurs into obscurity or goes unnoticed through folly, chaos, or naïveté. A love, therefore, that must be known to be felt. And its "unknowing" is a consequence of living in the hypnotic jungles of time and space, which, not so accidentally, makes possible the journey from *knowing into unknowing into knowing* that you call "life."

> No one knows how it all began, not even the dead, but everyone knows that it did.

The dead, as you can imagine, want you to sense what they can barely put into words so that you might "know" again sooner.

ONCE UPON A TIME

Consider if you will, perhaps as if from an altered state of consciousness, this love as just described. Imagine it as a translucent, iridescent light cascading upon you from above: all around you, arriving in unrelenting waves. Imagine it bathing you like sunshine, drenching you like rain, caressing you like the air, and illuminating everything. So enveloping that you can even breathe it into your lungs. This is also how to begin imagining God.

This love pierces you with its utter simplicity, energizes you, lifts your spirits, carries you, feels good, and makes you smile unceasingly as you bask in its overwhelming ecstasy. Where it comes from and how it began completely escape you, yet both seem so totally irrelevant. This love *"is"* as much as you *"are,"* undeniable, stunningly conscious, supremely confident, pure energy, and oriented toward joyful expansion. This love *is* God.

Imagine, too, that as you observe the physical world around you, which suddenly seems to be as translucent as the light of love illuminating it, you realize all "things" are *of* this love. Contrary to appearances, it's not that the love shines on or illuminates the objects of time, space, and matter but that these things are *it*, just as whitecaps on the tips of ocean swells, pushed by the wind, are part of the very ocean they roll over. You see that this love, in its flowing, can take on form, intelligently follow patterns, organize itself with purpose and intention, and *through* each adaptation experience itself as it couldn't before.

Then, as if struck by lightning, a new revelation hits you, and in total awe you consider that if everything around you is God, intelligence self-created within intelligence, dancing apparitions that can see one another, this must unequivocally mean *you* are exactly the same as what you are seeing. *You* are a part of this dance, a dancer yourself. You see you truly are of the Divine, by the Divine, for the Divine—*pure God,* a falling raindrop among countless others. God *self-reflecting* within time and space. You're part of the plan yet also now a plan maker as you choose new directions to aim your awareness. Discovering what is so obvious yet so unexpected: that you had to forget setting this all into motion in order to feel the passions your life has evoked, giving meaning to the journey. All is exactly as it should be. There is no other agenda. Nothing else has to happen. *You are God.*

What the Living Tell You

"Oh, come now, look around you!" People say stuff like, "Get real—time is running out, and God is losing patience. You were put on earth by His grace, and you will be judged by all of your choices, upon which God will decide whether you go to heaven or hell." Then they add, "God is merciful." Phew! Followed by "You live once, whether in a nation of feasts or famines, peace or war, as a male or female, briefly or for a hundred years, under democracy or dictatorship. That's just the way it goes. Fairness comes in the next world. Life is a test and all must have faith in God's love to pass it." God's love?

"Believe and you shall receive . . . Sow and you will reap
. . ." Phew! Better get on it! "Put the needs of others before your own . . . The devil makes work for idle hands
. . ." Oh dear! And should you find cracks or contradictions in the logic of this worldview, it's because "God
works in mysterious ways."

What the Dead See

Yet the living, your most immediate brothers and
sisters on this journey, in spite of all they still don't see,
are moved by love each day. There are strangers, even, who
would risk their joyful lives for yours if they found you
dangling from a bridge and they thought they might
be able to save you. The living are of good intent; they
actively, compassionately share concern for your well-
being, even as they expect God to "toast" those who
don't follow the rules. Weird.

People care about pretty much everything, everyone, always. It's just that they're also so busy believing
what they've been told, *and therefore manifesting it,* that
they genuinely have not yet noticed that in your gorgeous little planet's entire history, there's never been:

* A drought that didn't end,

* A storm that didn't clear,

* Lightning that didn't retreat,

* An earthquake that didn't still,

* A flood that didn't recede, or

* A plague that wasn't eventually, completely,
  and utterly overwhelmed by the healthy.

Now as a rule, the "dead" are not into odds, statistics, or gambling, but it doesn't take a genius to see that something's going on "down there," that the deck is clearly stacked, you've got friends in some very high places, and *none* of the "hard and mean" stuff was ever true. *Hit me, baby!*

The dead, with their advantage of perspective, see love everywhere. Individually and collectively, animate and inanimate. The living, not so much, even though it envelops them. They're usually too distracted by the illusions that, for now, speak louder to them than love.

After all, you can't eat a hug, nor can kindness shelter you from a storm. The dead, however, are beginning to see the connection. That through love—not in an instant, but applied consistently over time—the illusions can be tamed, managed, and harnessed, ultimately setting a stage where both coexist to create a spectacular new kind of platform for human expression and the joy of being. The goal is not to manipulate, defeat, or transcend time and space but to understand that *your* illusions within them are the extension of your own directed energy, *exactly* like an arm or leg. The sooner you see this, the sooner you can understand them, change them, and enjoy your time among them.

> **The dead, with their advantage of perspective, see love everywhere.**

THE LOVE GAMES

Love is the way. Love came first, and it's still there to see. From love the illusions "descended." Mistaking the illusions for reality keeps you from seeing your power over them—from seeing that you are *of* love, not *of* them. Only truth frees you. Therefore the path through the illusions to love, from the material world to an ethereal world brought down to earth, is through . . . *the truth.* Sound kind of familiar? Not through a person or savior? What savior? All are of God; all are saviors. No, it's through the truth about time, space, matter, and their origins. It will indeed set you free.

Holy smokes, not to sound religious, but these metaphors have too long been misconstrued. The whole Adam and Eve thing in the Garden of Eden, biting into the apple, was about *spiritual* beings on the *dreamscape of earth* reaching a tipping point in their growing misunderstanding of what was "real" and what was "illusion," to the degree that they actually bit into *the illusion* of an apple (because every*thing* is illusionary) as if it were real, thereby making it real to them! The apple then became something to contend with, just as the illusions of the world are now something to contend with rather than being seen as mere illusions.

Not at all a bad thing, not a "fall from grace"—except for how it's been portrayed by religion—but an awesome thing because then the games could begin. A full-blown '60s-style lovefest could (and did) commence within the illusions and everyone would (and did) begin *progressing* through truth toward love and their re-mastery over all *things*—"on earth, as it is in heaven" or, again, with "dominion over all *things*." Seeing themselves as the Creators they really are and thereby purposely, deliberately, excitedly, joyfully living upon this oasis among the stars with glad hearts, happy feet, and smiling faces, in love with everyone, everywhere, always.

So, excusing the frailty of words, perhaps you can now see that *love is the way,* the only way; it makes everything possible. And for those life adventurers now in the throes of this "love game," working their way to consciously expressing their divinity *within the illusions,* presently caught between a rock and a hard place, between hugs and food—in other words, adventurers like you—*truth is the path.*

It's Already Begun

You've been there, when . . .

Nothing made sense, *except for life's beauty.*

Nothing made sense, *except for how much you loved someone.*

Nothing made sense, *except for how much someone loved you.*

Nothing made sense, *except that you just knew that it must make sense, damn it!*

And through these cracks the light got in. Seeing the obvious, questioning the contradictions, and noticing how others seemed to live under very different rules with very different results, the sleeping giant began to awaken. Right on time.

When there was pain, sadness, illness, or lack, truth was summoned. Truth, however, that at first would inevitably contradict the things you believed in, that had brought about the pain to begin with! If the truth had been present in the beginning, there'd have been no suffering. And until you were ready to embrace the truth, cycles of painful or uncomfortable experiences repeated. Finally, too weary to continue, you surrendered, ready to let go rather than face further insult, only to find that when your resistance dropped, your heart opened, love poured in, tears turned happy, and you were lifted into a higher love orbit than ever before.

TAKING IT FROM HERE

Want more love, now, today? Fearlessly see more truth, in spite of appearances, no matter how much it threatens what you've been comforted by so far. Brace yourself. Love unimaginable awaits those who still, now, find "safe harbor" in lies:

"Safe Harbor" Lies

1. People are mean.
2. God decides who gets what when.
3. Life is a test, or life is not fair.
4. Materialism corrupts.
5. I want to be loved for who I am.

Likely Cover-Up

1. I am mean; others are my excuse.
2. I am not worthy.
3. I have no control and no responsibility.
4. I don't like being human/alive.
5. I resist life and I fear challenge.

Liberating Yet Scary Truth

1. I can and have to change first.

2. I am already good enough.

3. I accept full responsibility.

4. Money is pure spirit.

5. Bring it on!

Go for love. Dare to see the greater truths. There will always be justifications for every point in the first list, but they are fleeting and narrow. Whether deliberately or through nature's natural balancing act, however, gradual and subtle changes in your life will eventually deliver you to love's door. Take the bait. Don't wait. Seek the simple truth in all matters. Choose to expand your thinking, otherwise new circumstances brought about under your confusion (TBT) will do so for you.

THE UPWARD SPIRAL

With every success you're emboldened. With every surprise you become wiser. You laugh more, work less, play longer, feel better. And then something peculiar happens. The larger your manifestations become, the smaller are your succeeding desires. You no longer have to justify yourself. You start to change from the inside out. Yet successes continue; even as you want less, you get more. This is how abundant life is. Your priorities begin to shift. Everything seems so easy. You arrive on a plateau that confirms it's not the material things that bring you the most joy but the pursuit of them. And not because of what the pursuit promised, but for all that it didn't—the hidden gifts: new challenges, fears, and enemies. These were your greatest gifts! *Gifts* because they were met, faced, and befriended. They became the milestones of each journey and what you recall with the greatest fondness. You are not the same person you once were, yet you are; the world also seems to have changed, but it hasn't. Life suddenly makes sense and you want to live forever.

> Nothing made sense, *except for how much you loved someone.*

SELFISH SERVICE

As the expanse of your worldview broadens, you become aware of dreams you didn't earlier know to dream and love you didn't earlier know to give, and being of service and making a difference in the lives of others suddenly become what you most want to do. You're humbled not only that you have this opportunity, but that you can now see it. You cry happy tears almost daily. You physically feel lighter, as if you could float. You spiritually feel love in an entirely new way, not as a choice but as a channel for something far greater. You judge nothing because you see yourself in everything. You blame no one because blame is the evasion of responsibility. Animals are drawn to you. Trees communicate with you. Rainbows follow you on land. Dolphins follow you at sea. The unseen becomes visible, and there is not a spot in space that isn't filled and gurgling over with God, love, perfection, acceptance, and, most surprisingly, you—paintbrush in hand.

Yet with truth flowering before your very eyes all the more each day, a lingering sadness nags at your heart. You realize that this unbridled love is always, everywhere, even now as you read these words. Yet there are so many who do not see or feel it. Their lives and experiences seem to be polar opposites of the good and love you now feel. Your life is perfect except for this new sadness, which leads to desire. Those things you once wanted for yourself, most of which you already have, you now want for others. The things they want for themselves, you want for them. What you most want, selfishly, is to ease their pain and lighten their load.

And still, even more love, more glory, more opportunity shower down upon you.

The Shocking Perfection

As you think about those who do not share in the joy that you know is there for them, and as you take action to correct this imbalance, you discover the unthinkable . . . that many of their minds are closed *by choice!* That, when offered new ideas to think and choose from, *most choose the old!* They're blinded by their illusions and trapped by their fears—resistant, dogmatic, and unbending.

And then it hits you. You were once where they are, yet you found your way to the truth. And in hindsight you realize that you once needed to be where you were so that you could be pushed through it to where you now are. You also realize that your path and the enlightenment that followed were inevitable; it's the path of all in time and space. And so you also suddenly realize that just as you once chose to go through all you went through, with your own closed heart and mind, to eventually stand in the love you've found today, *so, too, are they on their own custom-designed pilgrimage to reach the same love you've found.* You see the perfection. It's so astonishing. Totally shocking. Utterly perfect. Everyone is where they most *want* to be; everyone's living their dreams, right now, even when they claim otherwise, even when it hurts, which is exactly what will eventually lead everyone home to more truth, more light, more love. Just as it's done for you.

Not that you won't lavish yourself on serving others; the idea of reaching those who have not yet been reached, *who are ready or nearly ready,* of creating ripples of good that roll throughout eternity, is far too irresistible. You will never let a moment go by without your hands and arms fully extended for the chance to lift others higher into the light. But gone will be the days of *selfless* service, self-denial, or self-sacrifice. No longer saddened and dragged down by the chaos in the minds of others, you will no longer be disappointed by those who need more time. And never again will you put off your own happiness when those you love choose to be unhappy. Instead, you will honor all that speaks to your heart and shine your light for the joy of it, for the good it will do you and thereby others, and because your dreams are yours for a reason: to lead you forever more into greater and greater love.

THE FINAL FRONTIER

There was a time in space on earth when it was believed that violence was the only way to exert control, live deliberately, and claim what was rightfully yours. Accordingly, evidence appeared to those who believed. And for a very long time, few, if any, *thought* otherwise.

There was a time when it was believed that worshipping the correct gods or idolizing the right prophets was the only way to successfully rule an empire; just look at ancient Egypt, Greece, Rome, *and most of the world today.* Accordingly, evidence appeared to those who believed. And for a very long time, few, if any, *thought* otherwise.

There was a time when it was believed that slavery, dishonesty, or intimidation was necessary to be economically successful in the world. Accordingly, evidence appeared to those who believed. And for a very long time, few, if any, *thought* otherwise.

There was a time when it was believed that men were superior to women, certain skin tones were better than others, or certain nationalities, cultures, or values were superior to others. Accordingly, evidence appeared to those who believed. And for a very long time, few, if any, *thought* otherwise.

Look to life's beauty for truth. And look to what hurts for its beauty.

None of these views were ever true, except to those who chose to believe in them. They were and are fleeting paradigms that briefly became self-evident, causing great pain until giving way to greater truths. You have within you the faculty to discern from infinite possibilities the truth you need to live a happy and fulfilling life today. To deduce what you need—that you are of God, you chose time and space, you knew what you were doing, it will all make sense one day, and to really get your groove on and have the time of your life, seek comfort in knowing:

1. Everything is God,

2. Thoughts become things, and

3. Love is all.

You are adored.

From a Dearly Departed

Dear Wedge—

I've never cried as much as I have here. Or laughed.

I thought I knew what to expect when I died—you know, either "God, judgment, a few deceased relatives" or "lights out, game over, absolute nothingness"—but I had no idea. Nothing could have prepared me for all I've found. How the whole world had it so wrong is beyond me.

How is it that our mere existence alone didn't prove to us there's intelligence in the Universe? That the whole place has a purpose, that life is good, that people are awesome?

As if there was something to risk in believing what's clearly obvious.

If I had had just an inkling of the truth about life and what I now know while I was alive, things would have been so different for me! Imagine living amid the all-or-nothing romance of time and space while learning how to change what you don't like, add more of what you do, and never be afraid of anything! Where everything is so precious, ephemeral, and fantastic! Where there is so much love, love, love, everywhere, always.

Why didn't I see it then? If I had known what I hope to convey to you, the magnanimous nature of reality, my confidence and optimism would have soared and I would have been unstoppable instead of constantly wondering about and searching for what was missing in me and what was wrong with the world.

Nothing is wrong, dear Wedge! You are gorgeous, life is beautiful, and everything is exactly as it should be. In the twinkling of an eye this will all be so clear to you, too, once your life is over. Except then it will be over. Don't wait, Wedge. Go, live, and be the precious wonder that you are! Dance, sing, follow your heart, and know you are provided for. You are loved. You are where you most wanted to be, with those you most wanted to be with, doing the kinds of things you most wanted to be doing, and with infinite possibilities to do even more.

Of course, you still have unfulfilled dreams, challenges, and things you want to change! That's why you're there! To step up and move toward them, to go where you've never been, and to think what you've never thought. Let the serendipities of these goals and how they coincide so perfectly with your spiritual growth be evidence that this entire odyssey of life was and is divinely inspired, and thus at any time going forward you can count on divine intervention—your own!

It's all so clear here: that life on earth is an ascension process, that everything you learn lifts you higher. That no matter what happens next, because it does you will be able to love more—someone else or yourself, same-same. That giving love eventually becomes an even greater need than receiving love, an addiction that afflicts all really old souls. And that this transformation is possible because we chose to "risk all," going where we could not lose, fail, or be made less but where we thought we could!

Therein lies our test, Wedge, a test of perceptions: of what to focus on, of what to believe in, in spite of appearances, while remembering that whatever does show up is a symbol of what we understand and of what we don't. Look to life's beauty for truth. And look to what hurts for its beauty.

You couldn't be more worthy of all your heart now desires, dear Wedgie, or more likely to get it.

Dancing on top of the world, drinking hot cocoa, with masses of affection for you—

Dolmar

Epilogue

It wasn't easy to write this book. The dead cooperated, but will its readers?

If the truth has been shared here, as I believe it has, you might wonder, as I have, why it hasn't been shared so explicitly before. Actually, much of it has; the recommended reading list in the appendix will soon show you that. But a lot of what I've addressed, others haven't. Why?

I think there are two reasons:

1. Few understand the absolute degree to which we are all the eyes and the ears of the Universe, *literally* "particles" of God come alive. And/or,

2. Some of what I shared might be extremely offensive to those who are not ready (or who don't want) to hear it.

I don't mind the first reason—obviously, it's very self-serving—but I cringe over the second.

Still, if it wasn't me, sooner or later someone else would have excitedly shared what's going on. The truth is the truth and it's going to come out. Moreover, how other people react to a message is about them, not the message. And finally, there's just too much good to come from the truth, the world over, for people who *are* ready, and their numbers are now increasing every day, exponentially. Droves *are* finally waking up, it's *that time* in our civilization's evolution, and they want to be given permission to go within and discern what their life is really about. I've offered a sort of road map. But I caution that you not accept any of what I've written until you've weighed it with your own feelings, deductions, and life experiences. Please, always, above all else, ask the hard questions, see what shows up, and then follow your heart and mind to uncover the treasures of truth that await you.

In summary of all that I've shared, being as concise as possible, you now stand at a major crossroads that every life adventurer eventually comes to. To believe that life is *awesome . . .*

a. All of the time,

b. Some of the time, or

c. None of the time.

Before you choose, let me ask: *How good was "some of the time" working for you?*

Once you can wrap your head around "a" as the answer—not that it will always be easy, but you didn't sign up for "easy"—not only will your life blast off and your joys multiply, but you will be a light in the darkness helping to lift all higher.

There's a new "sheriff" in town (not me), and while no one likes change, if—or better, when—you join the party, a wildly different world order awaits in which respect, cooperation, creativity, and love will blossom in ways we can't now comprehend.

However you feel about what you've been reading, about me, or about yourself, you are adored. At a minimum, the dead and I wish for you to know of your immortality and your natural-born abilities to live deliberately and to create consciously.

Until our paths cross again, perhaps at one big party "in the sky," may all that you now wish for be the least you receive—as I know it shall be.

By the way, the new sheriff is you.

Recommended
Reading

If you're now as curious as I once was to find out "Who else thinks like this?", here are the books that started showing up in my life that gave me the most peace, confirming my own thoughts and suspicions about life and reality. They're listed here in no particular order, except for the first, which is just one book of a series that rocked my world almost 35 years ago. Whether you seek these titles out, or allow others to find you, if you have questions and *insist* upon answers, one way or another you'll be reached by the truth.

***The Nature of Personal Reality* by Jane Roberts**
Like all her Seth books (and they're all outstanding), this one is very deep, objective, and even a bit

complex, but I consider Seth to be the "granddaddy of them all."

Discover the Power Within You: A Guide to the Unexplored Depths Within by Eric Butterworth
Awesome clarity. Extremely inspirational! Lots of biblical and Christian references, but explained as I believe they were originally meant, without the religious spin.

Siddhartha by Hermann Hesse
Profound wisdom in a timeless, world-famous story.

The Game of Life and How to Play It by Florence Scovel Shinn
Very simple and powerful advice, written in the 1920s. Easy reading for any age.

Life and Teaching of the Masters of the Far East (six-volume set) by Baird T. Spalding
Mind-bending! Volumes 1 and 2 are as adventurous as they are inspirational.

Illusions: The Adventures of a Reluctant Messiah and Jonathan Livingston Seagull by Richard Bach
Exhilarating, fun, and easy to read. These two novels are on almost everyone's list for good reason!

Journeys Out of the Body by Robert Monroe
The classic on out-of-body experiences.

Life after Life: The Investigation of a Phenomenon— Survival of Bodily Death by **Raymond A. Moody Jr. and Elisabeth Kübler-Ross**

> The classic on life after life and near-death experiences.

Conversations with God: An Uncommon Dialogue by **Neale Donald Walsch**

> Each of the books in this series is a mind-blower. They're also very easy and fun to read.

Emmanuel's Book: A Manual for Living Comfortably in the Cosmos by **Pat Rodegast and Judith Stanton**

> The entire series of Emmanuel books offers gentle yet powerful reminders of how angelic we all are. Wonderful.

Ramtha: The White Book by **Ramtha**

> Very friendly, powerful, and inspirational. Another easy read and one of the most powerful of all the titles listed here.

The Prophet by **Kahlil Gibran**

> Insight into life's most basic truths. Another perennial, international bestseller.

The Science of Getting Rich by **Wallace D. Wattles**

> If you've ever thought you might like wealth, you'll love this. A truly unique and encouraging perspective.

Messages from Michael by **Chelsea Quinn Yarbro**

> Very "out there," yet ringing of truth and containing revolutionary material I've not thought of or heard

of elsewhere. Helps me to be less critical of others and more patient with myself.

Atlas Shrugged and The Fountainhead by Ayn Rand
Although Ayn Rand was an agnostic/atheist, her books are extremely spiritual in that she considered herself a "man worshiper" and she reveled in the glory of life and our ability to have dominion over it all. Her epic novels are spellbinding, romantic, and deeply philosophical, and her talent is off the charts.

The Secret (DVD and book) by Rhonda Byrne
I'm grateful to have been one of the featured teachers in this outstanding documentary on the law of attraction. It's as inspirational as it is enlightening.

Acknowledgments

Writing is a tiny bit like giving birth to children, although my wife would not likely agree. In a single moment, what had never existed suddenly does. And unless or until you hit delete, those words may outlast you. Yikes . . . because like children, you tend to think that every single one of yours is the most beautiful, precious thing in the world, even though you may be the only one who thinks so.

I'd therefore like to tip my hat and share deep gratitude for my amazing editors in this work, Patty Gift and Anne Barthel, for both knowing when to encourage me, and for having the mettle to tell me when to stop, delete, or not even think about it! And for, at times, showing me what I really meant, in words I couldn't find. Your enthusiasm, empathy, street smarts, and skill are what every author dreams of one day having on his team, and I am happy our paths have crossed.

About the Author

Mike Dooley is a former PriceWaterhouseCoopers international tax consultant turned entrepreneur. He's the founder of a philosophical Adventurers Club on the Internet that's now home to more than 600,000 members from 182 countries. His inspirational books emphasizing spiritual accountability have been published in 25 languages, and he was one of the featured teachers in the international phenomenon *The Secret*. Today Mike is best known for his free "Notes from the Universe" e-mailings, his social network postings, and his *New York Times* bestsellers *Infinite Possibilities: The Art of Living Your Dreams* and *Leveraging the Universe: 7 Steps to Engaging Life's Magic*. Mike lives what he teaches, traveling internationally to speak on life, dreams, and happiness.

To receive Mike's daily "Notes," visit www.tut.com.

Hay House Titles of Related Interest

We hope you enjoyed this Hay House book. If you'd like to receive our online catalog featuring additional information on Hay House books and products, or if you'd like to find out more about the Hay Foundation, please contact:

Hay House, Inc., P.O. Box 5100, Carlsbad, CA 92018-5100
(760) 431-7695 or (800) 654-5126
(760) 431-6948 (fax) or (800) 650-5115 (fax)
www.hayhouse.com® • www.hayfoundation.org

———

Published in Australia by: Hay House Australia Pty. Ltd.,
18/36 Ralph St., Alexandria NSW 2015
Phone: 612-9669-4299 • *Fax:* 612-9669-4144
www.hayhouse.com.au

Published in the United Kingdom by: Hay House UK, Ltd.,
The Sixth Floor, Watson House, 54 Baker Street, London W1U 7BU
Phone: +44 (0)20 3927 7290 • *Fax:* +44 (0)20 3927 7291
www.hayhouse.co.uk

Published in India by: Hay House Publishers India,
Muskaan Complex, Plot No. 3, B-2, Vasant Kunj, New Delhi 110 070
Phone: 91-11-4176-1620 • *Fax:* 91-11-4176-1630
www.hayhouse.co.in

———

Access New Knowledge.
Anytime. Anywhere.

Learn and evolve at your own pace
with the world's leading experts.

www.hayhouseU.com